Metaheuristics for Robotics

Optimization Heuristics Set

coordinated by
Nicolas Monmarché and Patrick Siarry

Volume 2

Metaheuristics for Robotics

Hamouche Oulhadj
Boubaker Daachi
Riad Menasri

WILEY

First published 2020 in Great Britain and the United States by ISTE Ltd and John Wiley & Sons, Inc.

ISTE Ltd
27-37 St George's Road
London SW19 4EU
UK

www.iste.co.uk

John Wiley & Sons, Inc.
111 River Street
Hoboken, NJ 07030
USA

www.wiley.com

Library of Congress Control Number: 2019952981

British Library Cataloguing-in-Publication Data
A CIP record for this book is available from the British Library
ISBN 978-1-78630-380-6

Contents

Preface

Optimization deals with methods that make it possible to optimize the use, operation and performance conditions of a system, whether it is physical or related to human activity. Situated at the crossroads of several disciplines, namely applied mathematics, computer science and artificial intelligence, optimization makes it possible to quickly find a solution to numerous problems which would otherwise be more difficult to solve relying solely on restricted mathematical analysis.

Based on heuristics or even metaheuristics at a higher level, optimization methods provide operational solutions, which are not necessarily optimal solutions but eligible suboptimal solutions, so-called acceptable solutions, because they demonstrate the level of performance required to reach a goal without conflicting with associated constraints. A number of problems whose resolution is based on optimization methods can be provided as examples:

– in finance, tax optimization is a means to minimize legal taxation;

– in databases, query optimization makes it possible to improve the accessibility of shared data, in particular by reducing transaction time;

– in telecommunications networks, routing optimization is a method for finding suitable paths for data exchange;

– in robotics, optimization allows, to take just one example, the identification of the best configurations (joint variables) that a robot must undergo in order to efficiently perform a task;

– in computer science, optimizing the code of a program makes it possible to reduce the memory space occupied and to increase the convergence time.

The applications outlined above are inherently very complex, which raises the problems of implementing accurate mathematical methods that provide admissible solutions without having to mobilize huge computational resources. In these circumstances, we are limited to considering approximated solutions, which are suboptimal solutions, but acceptable, ones since they guarantee goal realization while satisfying constraints.

In this book, we will address issues specifically related to the field of medical robotics. The focus of the applications being considered is on trajectory planning for redundant manipulative arms (articulated robots) within the context of surgical gesture assistance, and robust control for effort compensation or physical assistance in disability situations (exoskeleton). These applications are presented in detail, with the aim of understanding with the utmost clarity the problems to be solved, as well as the choices made to find effective solutions within a reasonable time frame.

The methods developed make use of optimization metaheuristics, which are high-level abstraction algorithms. Unlike heuristics, which are computational processes, often informally and "individually" adapted to specific problems, metaheuristics are general algorithms applicable to a very wide range of optimization problems, without the need to resort to a fundamental modification of the structure of these algorithms. The methods studied and results achieved are commented on and presented in detail for each of the applications addressed. Although the proposed methods are developed within the context of their application to medical robotics, their generic nature allows them to be easily expanded to other optimization problems which do not necessarily fall within the same scope of application.

Hamouche OULHADJ
Boubaker DAACHI
Riad MENASRI
November 2019

Introduction

This work is part of a collection of books, published by ISTE and Wiley, devoted to metaheuristics and their applications. Known for being specific and particular algorithms, what practical interest do metaheuristics have to make them increasingly attractive to engineers, researchers and scientists from various areas interested in different fields of application? There are two important arguments that provide us with obvious answers: on the one hand, the scope of application of metaheuristics is constantly gaining momentum, without apparently being concerned with any limitations; on the other hand, these resolution methods possess a high level of abstraction, which makes them adaptable to a wide range of engineering problems. Furthermore, a small number of necessary adjustments that do not change the nature of algorithms are usually sufficient to solve new optimization problems without any particular links existing between them.

Moreover, metaheuristics belong to a particular class of algorithms, not always easy to configure and reserved for difficult optimization problems for which there are no accurate methods to solve them more efficiently. These problems are renowned for being complex and among them we can find problems whose mathematical models are not derivable; problems whose research space is too extended to exhaustively enumerate all feasible solutions, such as problems of a combinatorial nature or involving continuous decision variables; as well as any problem making use of highly noisy, erroneous or even incomplete data, which prove unsuitable for mathematical modeling. For all these categories of problems, we generally adopt approximated solutions belonging to the field of admissible solutions, which are capable of reaching a goal without violating constraints that might be *a priori* imposed.

In practice, there may be several existing solutions to an optimization problem, of which only one of these solutions is generally optimal. All others are suboptimal solutions, but are still eligible, so-called acceptable, solutions because they guarantee the completion of an objective without violating associated constraints. However, the notion of optimizing acceptability may appear to be overly abstract: how can the level of solution operability be identified when the level of appreciation of that solution may vary not only from one user to another, but also with the margin of error tolerated by each type of application? Clearly, there is no absolute answer to this question, because it is ultimately each individual who decides how to define the level of acceptability for a solution, based on individual needs and the quality of the results sought for the application to be addressed.

Are metaheuristics *deterministic* or *stochastic* algorithms? Providing a clear answer to this question is also not an easy task. In effect, while it is clear that metaheuristics are not deterministic algorithms, they are also not completely stochastic algorithms. In fact, they can be categorized halfway between these two families of algorithms, because solving an optimization problem by means of a metaheuristic systematically relies on a more or less random sampling process of the solution space.

When the algorithm is started, chance plays an important role in the process of finding solutions. Then, as the iterations progress, this randomness is progressively attenuated as we approach the final phase of the algorithm. Therefore, a metaheuristic will behave as a stochastic algorithm during initial iterations, and will asymptotically tend towards a greedy and deterministic algorithm during the last iterations. As we might expect, the accuracy of a metaheuristic lies in the right balance to be found between exploration phases, in which chance plays an important role, and the phases of intensification of solutions, also called phases of exploitation, in which randomness is reduced in order to focus only on potentially promising solutions. At the moment, there is no automatic parameterization method for these two search phases, whose respective weights generally depend on the type of application under study, the type of computational effort to be sustained and the type of results sought after.

Today, metaheuristics have become almost unavoidable in numerous areas of engineering due to the difficulties that have to be overcome to properly solve common optimization problems. These difficulties generally lie in the complex nature of the systems under study: the number of constraints and decision variables to be taken into account can be very high, computational times can be very long and non-differentiable objective functions can be highly multimodal or even too complex to be mathematically formalized with accuracy. The field of robotics is by nature a very broad field of application. In fact, these very relevant algorithms can be found in many applications of robotics:

– trajectory planning for mobile robots;

– robust control of portable robots for motion assistance;

– cooperation tasks between robots;

– vision in robotics.

In this book, we will focus more specifically on using metaheuristics for solving trajectory planning problems for redundant manipulative arms, as well as automatic control problems involving collaborative robots for assistance. These studies are conducted with a view to eventually exploiting the results within a clinical framework, within the context of surgical or physical assistance in order to compensate for efforts or to increase motor capabilities in performing a task.

With regard to trajectory planning, the difficulties raised are related to the redundant nature of the robot being used (the manipulative arm with several degrees of freedom), the nature of the environment in which the robot evolves (the environment cluttered with obstacles, uncertainties about the environment, etc.) and of course the complexity of the task at hand (the level of accuracy required, the time allowed to perform this task, the amount of motor power needed in order to minimize consumed energy and avoid sudden movements which could deteriorate the mechanical structure of the robot). All of these parameters can induce an excessively high number of decision variables and constraints to be taken into account.

For the control of collaborative robots (force-feedback robots designed for physical assistance in carrying out a task), the complexity of the problem resides in the almost infinite number of combinatory solutions to be tested before finding the proper values of control parameters. These must provide the desired optimal effort, within a reasonable time frame, without anachronistic movements that could endanger the person under assistance or present a risk of resonance that could deteriorate the mechanical structure of the robot. Since the automatic control system is designed to operate in an uncertain and dynamic environment, the task becomes more complex due to the servo control that operates in real time, in order to take into account external disturbances and the permanent evolution of input data (setpoints) over time.

We underline that the optimization issues studied in this book have been the subject of research carried out in collaboration between university laboratories and hospitals. Despite the practical and experimental aspect of this work, the methods developed are generic overall and can be generalized to other areas of application without requiring significant changes in the structure of the algorithms. Given this last point, these methods might be of particular interest to a very wide audience including students of robotics, algorithmics, applied mathematics and operational research, as well as engineers or teachers/researchers whose work deals with difficult optimization problems.

This book is organized into five chapters.

Chapter 1 is a general study which reviews the mathematical foundations needed for modeling optimization problem in order to solve them using numerical methods. A list of basic methods can be found therein, including comments and a great deal of information about their characteristics and properties. This chapter is essential for understanding the approaches developed in the following chapters to solve more complex medical problems.

Chapter 2 focuses on the application of metaheuristics in optimization problems related to robotics. Particular emphasis is placed on issues related to the fields of trajectory planning and automatic control. The challenges encountered, the difficulties that have to be overcome and the pertinence of metaheuristics for their solution in an approximate but sufficiently effective manner are described with the utmost concern for clarity. Most common general algorithms within these two areas of application are also presented in detail.

Chapter 3 is dedicated to the specific problem of trajectory planning for redundant manipulative arms. A resolution method based on a *bigenetic algorithm* (two genetic algorithms running in parallel) is presented in this chapter. Inspired by two-tier optimization problems, this method distinguishes two planning spaces: the Cartesian space, in order to control and guide the movements of the effector (terminal organ of the manipulative arm) in the work environment, and the joint space, in order to operate the different segments of the motorized arm. The coordination of the movements of the robot within these two spaces is ensured by the collaboration of the two genetic algorithms. Each of these two algorithms uses its own decision variables and optimizes its own *objective* function by exploring its limited planning space (Cartesian space or joint space exclusively). Nonetheless, the decision-making processes of the two algorithms are achieved through interaction by permanently exchanging their data. In this way, the results of one of the algorithms are also exploited by the other, in order to strengthen or correct its own decisions.

Chapter 4 focuses on a particular aspect of trajectory planning, i.e. how smooth curves are obtained (primitive and derived curves). Based on the results produced by the method outlined in Chapter 3, the objective is to complement the latter in order to simultaneously optimize the trajectory and the dynamic behavior of the robot. For this purpose, the planning of the trajectory is reformulated in the form of a constrained optimization problem, the resolution of which resorts to a metaheuristic combining a genetic algorithm with the *augmented Lagrangian* method.

Chapter 5 addresses the problems of state feedback control for collaborative robots. More specifically, the main topic will concern the exoskeleton, whose purpose is to increase motor skills when performing a task or for effort compensation in disability situations. The automated control system implements a *PID* controller. The goal is to find the optimal combination of the three actions of the controller, providing in real time the effort best suited to the needs of the assisted person:

– *proportional action*: the control error is multiplied by a gain K_p;

– *integral action*: the error is multiplied by a gain K_i;

– *derivative action*: the error is multiplied by a gain K_d;

The problem to be solved being combinatory by nature and using continuous variables, the difficulty lies in the almost infinite number of solutions to be tested to find the combination of parameters K_p, K_i and K_d that would produce the appropriate control torque. The second difficulty lies in the real-time operation of the *PID* control, in order to take into account the external disturbances and the continuous evolution of the work requested of the robot. To overcome all these difficulties, a metaheuristic based on an algorithm making use of swarm intelligence is developed. This metaheuristic is an adaptation of the particle swarm optimization (PSO) algorithm for the purposes of the application.

Finally, a general conclusion, given at the end of the book, briefly summarizes the problems studied and reviews the methods recommended for solving them appropriately. Development perspectives and avenues to be explored are also outlined to ultimately make use of the results in a clinical framework. This conclusion is followed by a list of bibliographic references that the reader can consult in order to deepen their understanding, if necessary, of the theoretical and practical concepts developed in this book.

Optimization: Theoretical Foundations and Methods

1.1. The formalization of an optimization problem

An optimization problem is usually equivalent to finding the global minimum $\check{x}$ of a function $f: E^n \rightarrow R$, which is defined on a subset E^n of the set R^n of the real numbers, such that $\check{x} \in E^n$ and $f(\check{x}) \leq f(x)$ for all x of E^n. This definition can be formalized as follows:

$$Arg \min \{f(x) \, / \, x \in E^n \subseteq R^n\} \tag{1.1}$$

It should be noted that any optimization algorithm designed for searching the global minimum of a function can also be applied to the search for the global maximum, by previously transforming the optimization problem into a minimization problem. The simplest transformation can be written as:

$$\varphi(x) = -f(x) \tag{1.2}$$

With formalization [1.1], the existence of constraints that could condition the problem to be solved is not taken into account. In this case, the set E^n covers the entire physical search space without any restriction. When integrating constraints, only solutions that comply with them should be taken into account. These solutions, known as achievable or admissible solutions, form a small restricted subset A^n, such that $A^n \subset E^n$. The classic formalization of such an optimization problem can be written as:

$$Arg\ min\ \{f(x)\ /\ x \in E^n \subseteq R^n\}$$
$$s.c. \begin{cases} h_i(x) = 0, i = 0, 1, \dots, n \\ g_i(x) \leq 0, i = 0, 1, \dots, m \end{cases} \qquad [1.3]$$

where functions $h_i(x)$ represent the constraints of equality and functions $g_i(x)$ represent the constraints of inequality. The above formalization can be very easily generalized to constraints $g_i(x) \geq 0$, by applying the transformation $\varphi_i(x) = -g_i(x)$.

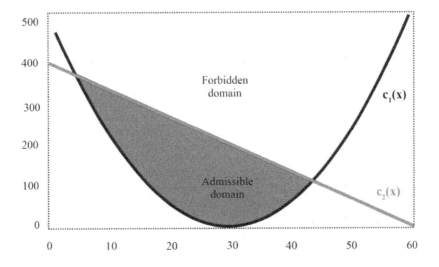

Figure 1.1. *Domain of admissible solutions and forbidden domain*

The constraints divide the research space into admissible and forbidden domains. The admissible domain includes all achievable solutions that do not violate constraints. The forbidden domain represents the complementary set, formed by non-achievable solutions, which do not comply with constraints. Figure 1.1 shows an example of a two-constraint problem $g_1(x) \geq 0$ and $g_2(x) \leq 0$, whose boundary curves $c_1(x)$ and $c_2(x)$ delineate the lower and upper boundaries of the admissible space.

The objective function of an optimization problem can be either unimodal or multimodal. These are also referred to as convex or non-convex problems. A typical example of a convex problem is one where the curve of the objective function has only one valley. In the presence of a curve with two or more valleys, the problem is called non-convex. Convex optimization problems are naturally less difficult to analyze and solve. Nevertheless, it is seldom the case in practice to be confronted with problems of this nature. Even in this favorable case, many false optima can be produced by noise. Under such conditions, the optimization problem may be undifferentiable or even biased when the global optimum is moved due to noise. In the absence of correction, this is obviously very annoying, because of the objective function that may no longer reflect the effective data of the problem to be solved. Figures 1.2–1.5 show examples of non-convex objective functions in the absence and presence of noise.

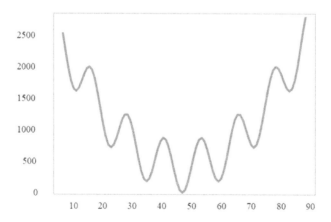

Figure 1.2. *1D multimodal objective function, in the absence of noise*

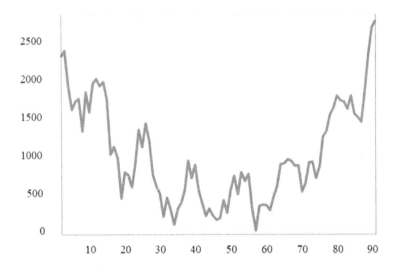

Figure 1.3. *1D multimodal objective function, in the presence of noise*

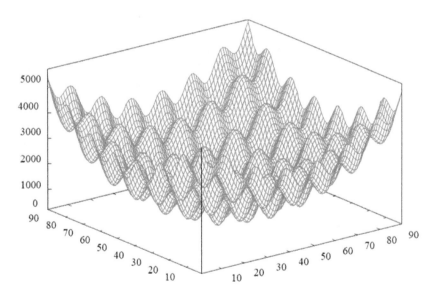

Figure 1.4. *2D multimodal objective function, in the absence of noise*

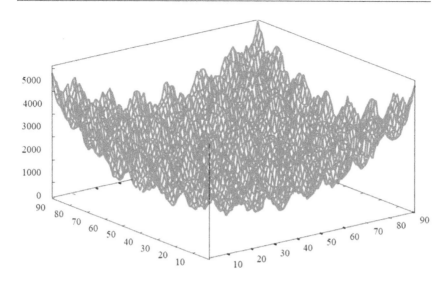

Figure 1.5. *2D multimodal objective function, in the presence of noise*

The global optimum of a constrained optimization problem is not invariably identical to the global optimum of the same problem in the absence of constraints. Figure 1.6 shows an example of a constrained optimization problem, whose global optimum is identical to that of the initial problem without constraints. This is not the case with the example in Figure 1.7, as the initial global optimum is no longer an acceptable solution to the constrained problem. Using resolution methods, based on the transformational approach, detailed hereafter, the landscape of the objective function of the constrained problem can change radically.

1.2. Constrained optimization methods

To solve a constrained optimization problem, two possible approaches can be considered: the direct approach and the indirect approach. The direct approach can be formalized as follows:

$$(P_X) = Arg \min_{x \in X} f(x) \qquad [1.4]$$

where $X = A^n \subset E^n$ represents the space of admissible solutions and $f : x \in E^n \rightarrow f(x) \in R$ is the objective function defined on a subset $E^n \subset R^n$, covering the admissible space and its complementary space known as the forbidden space.

This approach can prove very difficult in its implementation in situations where the admissible space is complex or difficult to circumscribe, especially when it is very small compared to the forbidden space.

In the indirect approach, the problem of constrained optimization is first transformed into an unconstrained problem, and then solved by making use of any unconstrained optimization method. This approach, also known as a transformational approach, is much more convenient to implement because it allows us to focus on the optimization process without having to worry about constraints, once formalized. Such an approach can be formalized as follows:

$$(P_Y) = Arg \min_{x \in Y} \varphi(x, r) \qquad [1.5]$$

where $Y = E^n \subseteq R^n$ is the global search set (including the admissible domain and the forbidden domain) and $\varphi(x, r)$ is a composite objective function, including constraints, such that:

$$\varphi : x \in E^n \rightarrow \varphi(x, r) = [f(x) + r.p(x)] \in R \qquad [1.6]$$

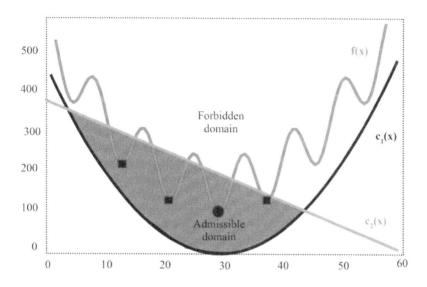

Figure 1.6. *Constrained optimization.* ■ *Local minima.*
● *Global minimum. For a color version of this figure, see*
www.iste.co.uk/oulhadj/metaheuristics.zip

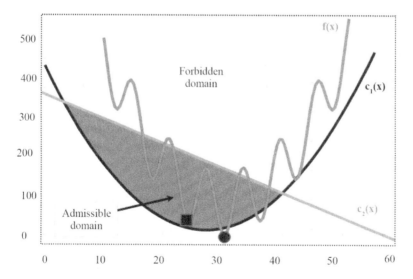

Figure 1.7. *Constrained optimization.* ■ *Global minimum in the presence of constraints.* ● *Global minimum in the absence of constraints. . For a color version of this figure, see www.iste.co.uk/oulhadj/metaheuristics.zip*

In expression [1.6], f is the objective function of the initial unconstrained problem, r is called the constraint penalty factor $x \in A^n$, which is generally a positive real to be adjusted, and p is the penalty function of the constraint violation, such that:

$$p : x \in E^n \rightarrow p(x) \in R \qquad\qquad [1.7]$$

Penalization plays an important role in transformation methods. However, it is inaccurate because it does not clarify the possible link between problems (P_X) and (P_Y) defined above. Therefore, the penalty may be accurate or inaccurate, depending on the degree of the link that may exist between the two problems (P_X) and (P_Y). By definition, it will be said that the penalty carried out in (P_Y) is accurate if the solutions of (P_X) are the solutions of (P_Y). Otherwise, the penalty will be said to be inaccurate. In this case, the link between problems (P_X) and (P_Y) is not necessarily missing. This link can, in fact, be asserted asymptotically by making the penalty factor r tend towards its limit, zero or infinity, in order to balance the weight of the penalty function, which is not always simple to build. In practice, we do not apply a rigid transformation with a single value of r, but a succession of small transformations by gradually making r tend to its limit, in order to reduce the risk of forming a badly conditioned problem:

– if r is too small, the influence of constraints is reduced; in this situation, the algorithm can easily converge towards a stationary point in the forbidden domain;

– if r is too large, it is the influence of the objective function of the initial unconstrained problem that is in turn reduced; in this case, the optimum of the constrained problem may correspond to a stationary point that is not necessarily a solution to the initial unconstrained problem;

– if r is far from its limits, the admissibility of the final solution produced cannot be guaranteed nor can we claim with certainty that the corresponding stationary point will be a stationary point of the initial unconstrained problem.

The most commonly used transformation methods are *Penalty* methods (in the sense of violating constraints) [CAR 61, FIA 68] and *Lagrange*'s methods [HES 69, POW 69, ROC 73], described further in this chapter.

1.2.1. *The method of Lagrange multipliers*

Optimization problems can be solved under equality constraints. The formalization of such a problem can be written as:

$$Arg\min\{\varphi(x,\lambda) = f(x) + \sum_{i=0}^{m}\lambda_i h_i(x); \ x \in E^n \subseteq R^n\} \quad [1.8]$$

where φ is the objective function of the problem integrating constraints, f is the objective function of the initial problem without constraints, the coefficients λ_i are Lagrange multipliers and h is the function modeling equality constraints.

1.2.1.1. *Necessary optimality conditions*

If $\check{x}$ is a desired solution, we can show that there exists a vector $\check{\lambda}$ such that the function $\varphi(x,\lambda)$ admits a first-order differential equal to zero at point $(\check{x},\check{\lambda})$:

$$\begin{cases} \dfrac{\partial\varphi(\check{x},\check{\lambda})}{\partial x_i} = \dfrac{\partial f(\check{x})}{\partial x_i} + \sum_{j=0}^{m}\check{\lambda}_j\dfrac{\partial h_j(\check{x})}{\partial x_i} = 0; \ i = 1,2,\dots,n \\ \dfrac{\varphi(\check{x},\check{\lambda})}{\partial\lambda_i} = h_i(\check{x}) = 0; \ i = 1,2,\dots,m \end{cases} \quad [1.9]$$

In a more compact form, it can be written that:

$$\nabla\varphi(\check{x},\check{\lambda}) = \nabla f(\check{x}) + \nabla h^T(\check{x})\check{\lambda} = 0 \ and \ h(\check{x}) = 0 \quad [1.10]$$

Note that this first-order condition is only a necessary optimality condition, which only informs of the possible existence of a local minimum in $\check{x}$. To complete this information, it is necessary to study the second-order differential:

– if $\dfrac{\partial^2 \varphi(\check{x},\check{\lambda})}{\partial x^2} > 0,$ the local extremum is a minimum;

– if $\dfrac{\partial^2 \varphi(\check{x},\check{\lambda})}{\partial x^2} < 0,$ the local extremum is a maximum;

– if $\dfrac{\partial^2 \varphi(\check{x},\check{\lambda})}{\partial x^2} = 0,$ higher   derivative   calculations   are required, given that the local extremum could be either a minimum or a maximum, or an inflection point.

1.2.1.2. *Necessary and sufficient conditions*

For single-variable functions, the necessary and sufficient conditions that guarantee a local minimum in $\check{x}$ can be written as:

$$\begin{cases} \dfrac{\partial \varphi(\check{x},\check{\lambda})}{\partial x} = \dfrac{\partial f(\check{x})}{\partial x} + \dfrac{\partial h^T(\check{x})\check{\lambda}}{\partial x} = 0 \ and \ h(\check{x}) = 0 \\ \dfrac{\partial^2 \varphi(\check{x},\check{\lambda})}{\partial x^2} = \dfrac{\partial^2 f(\check{x})}{\partial x^2} + \dfrac{\partial^2 h^T(\check{x})\check{\lambda}}{\partial x^2} > 0 \end{cases}$$ [1.11]

By generalizing this formalization to multi-variable functions, the necessary and sufficient conditions that guarantee a local minimum in $\check{x}$ can be written as:

$$\begin{cases} \nabla\varphi(\check{x},\check{\lambda}) = \nabla f(\check{x}) + \nabla h^T(\check{x})\check{\lambda} = 0 \ and \ h(\check{x}) = 0 \\ x^T H_\varphi(\check{x},\check{\lambda})x = H_f(\check{x}) + H_h^T(\check{x})\check{\lambda} > 0 \end{cases}$$ [1.12]

where $H_\varphi(\check{x},\check{\lambda})$, $H_f(\check{x})$ and $H_h(\check{x})$ respectively represent the Hessians of functions $\varphi(x,\lambda)$, $f(x)$ and $h(x)$ at points $\check{x}$ and $\check{\lambda}$. For any function $g : A^n \to R$, defined on a subset A^n of the set R^n and with values in the set R, the Hessian of g is a square matrix, which can be written as:

$$H(x) = \begin{bmatrix} \dfrac{\partial^2 g(x)}{\partial x_1^2} & \cdots & \dfrac{\partial^2 g(x)}{\partial x_1 \partial x_n} \\ \vdots & \ddots & \vdots \\ \dfrac{\partial^2 g(x)}{\partial x_n \partial x_1} & \cdots & \dfrac{\partial^2 g(x)}{\partial x_n^2} \end{bmatrix}$$ [1.13]

With second derivatives corresponding to continuous functions, some calculations can be avoided by virtue of the Schwarz theorem:

$$\frac{\partial^2 g(x)}{\partial x_i \partial x_j} = \frac{\partial^2 g(x)}{\partial x_j \partial x_i}$$ [1.14]

$H(x)$ is then a symmetrical square matrix.

1.2.2. *Method of the quadratic penalization*

This method was one of the first proposed to solve optimization problems with equality constraints. It was later extended to problems involving inequality constraints. The general form of the optimization problem can be written as:

$$Arg \min\{\varphi(x,\mu) = f(x) + \mu\|g(x)\|^2; \, x \in E^n \subseteq R^n\} \quad [1.15]$$

The value of the penalty parameter μ conditions the performance of the solving algorithm. If this parameter is not large enough, the algorithm will converge to a stationary point in the forbidden domain. If it is too large, it will increase the risk of shifting the optimum of the constrained problem to a stationary point that is not necessarily a solution to the initial unconstrained problem. As with most penalty methods, this dilemma is resolved by transforming the minimization problem into a succession of small minimization problems, by gradually increasing the value of the parameter μ in the interval $[V_{min}, V_{max}]$ over the iterations. The bounds V_{min} and V_{max} of this interval are usually quite problematic to find. Often, they are set empirically, depending on the application.

1.2.3. *Methods of interior penalties*

These methods are used to solve optimization problems with constraints of inequality. The constrained optimization problem is transformed into an unconstrained optimization problem of the form:

$$Arg\ min\{\varphi(x,\mu) = f(x) + \sum_{i=0}^{m}\mu_i P_i\big(g_i(x)\big); \ x \in E^n \subseteq R^n\}[1.16]$$

where $\varphi(x,\mu)$ represents the objective function of the problem under constraints, $f(x)$ is the objective function of the initial unconstrained problem, $P_i\big(g_i(x)\big)$ are the penalty functions of the violation of constraints $g_i(x)$, such that $P_i\big(g_i(x)\big) \geq 0 \ \forall \ x \in A^n$ and the coefficients $\mu_i > 0$ are penalty parameters.

Denoting by $g(x) \leq 0$ the set of the admissible points forming the domain of achievable solutions, the interior penalty approach makes penalties tend towards 0 far from the limits of the constraints, and towards infinity at the limits of constraints. The following functions represent examples of functions used in the interior penalty method:

$$\begin{cases} P(x) = \dfrac{-1}{g(x)} \\ P(x) = \dfrac{1}{[g(x)]^2} \\ P(x) = log\left(1 - \dfrac{1}{g(x)}\right) \end{cases} \qquad [1.17]$$

Interior penalty is also referred to as a barrier approach, because the penalty function forms an infinite barrier along the boundary of the admissible domain. Its implementation assumes that we are considering the space of admissible solutions from the start of the optimization algorithm. In order to be within this space at the beginning, a simple solution consists of randomly sampling the search space until a hook point is found where the algorithm will be started. This process, relatively easy to implement, may nonetheless prove to be very slow, as several tests may be required before a first drop-off point is found in the domain of admissible solutions. This is particularly true in the presence of an admissible space which is very small compared to the forbidden space. Since it requires a set of achievable parameters from the start of the algorithm, the barrier approach can prove difficult to implement. Nevertheless, it is very convenient because it has the advantage of guaranteeing the admissibility of the solutions found.

1.2.4. *Methods of exterior penalties*

Analogously to interior penalty, exterior penalty is proposed to solve optimization problems with inequality constraints. Moreover, the approach is based on the same transformation (see equation [1.16]). The difference lies in the fact that penalties are zero in the space of admissible points and positive when constraints are no longer satisfied, as in the following examples:

$$\begin{cases} P(x) = max(0, g(x)) \\ P(x) = [max(0, g(x))]^2 \\ P(x) = \max(\beta^{g(x)} - 1, 0) \end{cases} \qquad [1.18]$$

Exterior penalty has the advantage of being more flexible than interior penalty, because it does not impose any barrier to the search space, which indiscriminately covers the space of admissible solutions and the so-called forbidden complementary space. On the contrary, it does not offer any guarantee concerning the admissibility of the final solution found, as it may at best be located in the space of admissible points or simply near its boundary, on the side of the forbidden space.

1.2.5. *Augmented Lagrangian method*

The augmented Lagrangian method was initially proposed to overcome difficulties associated with ill-conditioning in quadratic penalization in order to optimally solve problems with equality constraints. The idea is to solve a series of minimization problems by progressively penalizing constraint violation. The problem to be solved is of the form:

$$Arg \min\{\varphi_{\lambda,\mu}(x) = f(x) + \lambda^T h(x) + \mu \|h(x)\|^2; \ x \in E^n \subseteq R^n\} \qquad [1.19]$$

where $\lambda = (\lambda_1, \lambda_2, \dots \lambda_n)$ is an estimate of the Lagrange multipliers and $\mu > 0$ is the penalty parameter. At every iteration k, an instance of the minimization problem is resolved with precision ε_k, and the Lagrange multipliers or the penalty parameter of iteration $k+1$ are updated:

– if the violation of constraints is less than a target value, the Lagrange multipliers are increased using the following formula:

$$\lambda_i^{k+1} = \lambda_i^k + \mu^k h_i(x) \qquad [1.20]$$

– otherwise, the penalty parameter is increased; a form of updating μ is:

$$\mu^{k+1} = \alpha \mu^k \qquad [1.21]$$

where $\alpha > 1$ depends on the application.

In its generalization to optimization problems with mixed constraints, several formalizations of the augmented Lagrangian method have been proposed. The most commonly used is:

$$Arg \min\{\varphi_{\lambda,\mu}(x) = f(x) + \lambda^T h(x) + \mu_1 \|h(x)\|^2 + \mu_2^T P(g(x))\}$$
$$x \in E^n \subseteq R^n$$
$$[1.22]$$

It can be observed that there are two penalty parameters: μ_1 and μ_2. As a general rule, μ_2 increases at each iteration when the function $P(g(x))$ is associated with an exterior penalty, and decreases in the case of an interior penalty, in order to approach the boundary of the admissible space, if necessary. The parameter μ_1 and the Lagrange multipliers λ are updated to reflect the violation of constraints, as in the augmented Lagrangian approach associated with the quadratic penalization of the equality constraints: if the last solution is sufficiently admissible, then λ is increased and μ_1 is kept constant; otherwise, λ is kept constant and μ_1 is increased.

1.3. Classification of optimization methods

Numerical optimization methods rely on iterative algorithms, whose parameters usually require adjustment before achieving the desired performance. This step of adjusting parameters is akin to a learning step, which improves the accuracy of the algorithm according to the trial and error method. For this purpose, a training dataset is used in accordance with the application under study. The more test data we have, the more we can improve the parameters and performance of the algorithm. Figure 1.8 shows the overall process of adjusting the performance of an optimization algorithm by way of refining its parameters based on the trial and error method.

Optimization methods can be categorized according to several criteria. In view of the approach used to explore the solution space, two families of methods can be distinguished: deterministic methods and stochastic methods. The common property of deterministic methods is to systematically exploit the results of each iteration in order to focus the search on promising areas during the following iterations. These are referred to as exploitation methods. Conversely, stochastic methods make possible the exploration of search areas not necessarily favorable, which over the course of iterations may prove to be potential areas to reach the global optimum. Known as exploration methods, they provide better coverage of the search space. On the other hand, they are slower because they require higher numbers of evaluations of the objective function.

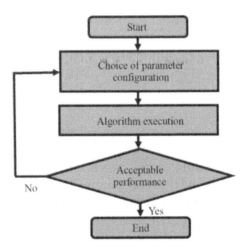

Figure 1.8. *Refinement of the performance of an algorithm*

1.3.1. *Deterministic methods*

These methods ensure a good local search. They share the following common properties:

– they require relatively few evaluations of the objective function;

– under the same initialization conditions, they always lead to the same final solution;

– they have the disadvantage of getting stuck in the first local minimum visited.

Deterministic methods can be divided into two groups: zeroth-order methods, or those without derivatives, and first-order methods, with derivatives. Zeroth-order methods, also known as *heuristic* or *geometric* methods, take advantage of the values of the objective function, extracted at sampling times of the research space. First-order methods, called *analytical* or *descent* methods, require in addition the computation of the gradient of the objective function. Figure 1.9 presents the most commonly used deterministic methods.

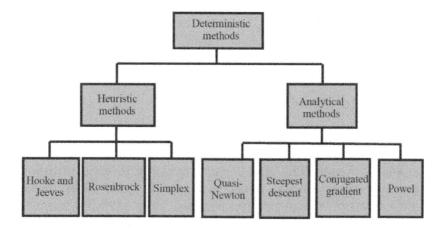

Figure 1.9. *Some deterministic methods*

1.3.1.1. *Heuristics*

These methods explore the space of solutions through a series of trials in order to find the most favorable points. The most common are the Hooke and Jeeves local variation methods [CHE 99], the Rosenbrock method [RAO 96] and the Simplex method [NEL 65].

1.3.1.2. *Analytical methods*

These methods, which are based on differentiation operations, have the advantage of accelerating the convergence of algorithms, because the computation of the gradient gives information about the direction to follow in order to find the best local solution. On the other hand, they are very sensitive to noise, as they easily get stuck in the first local minimum visited. Worse still, they might become inapplicable when the objective function is not differentiable, which is frequent for many real optimization problems. The most commonly used analytical methods are the *quasi-Newton* methods [CUL 94], the *Greater Slope* method [KOW 68], the *Conjugated Gradient* method [CUL 94, PRE 92] and the *Powel* method [POW 65].

1.3.2. **Stochastic methods**

These are methods involving no differentiation, which evaluate the objective function based on randomly sampling the search space. The risk of getting stuck in local minima, especially those due to noise, is lower. On the other hand, they converge more slowly, because they require a more significant number of evaluations of the objective function. In addition, they are weaker in terms of the reproducibility of results, as they can produce a different solution at each new execution, even when the initialization data are the same. Among existing stochastic methods, methods can be distinguished between those that perform systematic exploration and those that alternate exploration phases with exploitation phases. Purely stochastic methods are called *Monte Carlo* methods. The latter form a family of specific methods, much more subtle but more complex in their implementation, called *metaheuristics*. Figure 1.10 presents some examples of common stochastic methods.

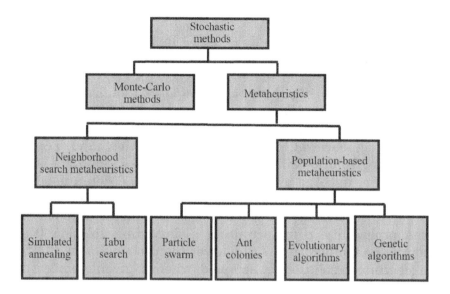

Figure 1.10. *Some stochastic methods*

1.3.2.1. *Monte Carlo methods*

Monte Carlo methods are based on random sampling of the search space, in which every point has the same probability of being reached. As a general rule, they are quite simple to implement. However, they converge more slowly, because they require a very large number of visits to the objective function before getting as close to the optimal solution as possible.

1.3.2.2. *Metaheuristics*

Alternating phases of exploration with phases of exploitation, metaheuristics are capable of reaching the global optimum, especially with non-convex optimization problems. These methods can be divided into two classes: neighborhood search metaheuristics and population-based metaheuristics. In the rest of this section, we describe each of these two families of methods.

1.3.2.2.1. Neighborhood search metaheuristics

The most commonly used neighborhood search metaheuristics are simulated annealing (SA) [KIR 83, SIA 14, TAL 09] and tabu search (TS) [GLO 89, GLO 90, HU 92, SIA 14, TAL 09]. They rely on a single solution that is made to progress over time, perturbating it locally in a random way. These metaheuristics differ in the way they explore the local neighborhood of the current solution and accept degrading solutions if necessary, in order to get out of a local minimum. In SA, a temperature parameter T, determined at the start of the algorithm, decreases over the iterations in order to tend to 0. The value of this parameter depends on the probability p for accepting a degrading solution (the lower the temperature T, the lower the probability p). In TS, a degrading solution is accepted when a given number of local search attempts have not achieved any improvement of the current solution. In order to avoid recycling an already visited minimum, TS forbids traveling backwards to the latest solutions visited. To this end, a tabu list containing attributes of these solutions is kept up to date throughout the execution of the optimization algorithm.

Neighborhood search metaheuristics are relatively simple to implement, but their performance depends heavily on the initialization step. To get as close as possible to the global solution, it may be necessary to increase the number of iterations of the algorithm or to restart it several times with new initialization data.

1.3.2.2.2. Population-based metaheuristics

Population-based metaheuristics (particle swarm optimization, ant colonies, evolutionary algorithms, etc.) enable several solutions to progress in parallel by making them cooperate over time, similarly to a population of intelligent individuals operating in groups to accomplish a complex task, which they do not know how to accomplish properly outside of the group. These methods differ according to the cooperation mechanisms implemented in the algorithms. These can be based on direct exchanges of information between individuals in the population, such as in particle swarm optimization [KEN 95, TAL 09, SIA 14] and bee colonies [TAL 09, SIA 14], or indirect exchanges via the modification of the external environment of the population, such as in ant colonies [GOS 89, DOR 96, TAL 09, SIA 14]. There are also much more subtle mechanisms for solutions to make progress in parallel. These latter aim to strengthen individual capabilities within a population over time, in order to improve solutions by means of mutation and crossover operations of individuals of that population, as in evolutionary algorithms [PRE 90, REC 94, FOG 94, KAS 95, TAL 09, SIA 14] and genetic algorithms [HOL 75, MIC 94, KOZ 95, TAL 09, SIA 14].

Compared to neighborhood search metaheuristics, population-based metaheuristics provide better coverage of the search space, thus achieving better results. On the other hand, they are relatively slower and more difficult to implement because of cooperation mechanisms that can be somewhat complex to implement in an algorithm. To speed up algorithms, the most popular solution relies on the parallelization of processes, by executing programs on multi-core computing architectures.

1.4. Conclusion

This introductory chapter on optimization methods is not exhaustive. The objective is to understand the general problem of optimization, in order to best address the following chapters devoted to case studies. The main methods used are succinctly outlined, their general operating principles are explained, and their strengths and disadvantages are recalled. It will be understood that the value of the parameters of an optimization algorithm has a significant impact on the results, performance relying heavily on the accuracy of adapting these parameters to each application. At the moment, there is no optimization method fully non-parameterized that is absolutely safe to produce high-performance results across all applications. For problematic cases of high complexity, satisfactory results can only be obtained at the expense of hybridizing methods [MOH 97], in order to take advantage of their complementarities.

The choice of an optimization method is also not an easy operation. Given the multitude of methods proposed, common sense recommends that we first use easy-to-program methods. In the event of failure or poor results, following multiple attempts to adapt the algorithm implemented, it is possible to experiment with more complex methods, which are generally slower and more difficult to program. The right choice of an optimization method is in any case a compromise between the quality of the results sought after and the computational effort.

1.5. Bibliography

[BOX 71] BOX M.J., DAVIES D., SWANN W.H., *Techniques d'optimisation non linéaire,* Entreprise Moderne d'Édition, 1971.

[BRE 73] BRENT R.P., *Algorithms for Minimization without Derivatives,* Prentice Hall, 1973.

[CAR 61] CAROLL C.W., "The created response technique for optimizing nonlinear restrained systems", *Operational Research,* vol. 9, pp 169–184, 1961.

[CHE 99] CHERRUAULT Y., *Optimisation : Méthodes locales et globales,* Presses Universitaires de France, 1999.

[CUL 94] CULIOLI J.C., *Introduction à l'optimisation,* Ellipses, 1994.

[DOR 96] DORIGO M., MANIEZZO V., COLORNI A., "Ant system : optimization by a colony of cooperating agents", *IEEE Transactions on Systems, Man, and Cybernetics, Part B: Cybernetics*, pp. 29–41, 1996.

[FIA 68] FIACCO A.V., MCCORMICK G.P., *Nonlinear Programming Sequential Unconstrained Minimization Techniques*, John Wiley & Sons Ltd., 1968.

[FLE 80] FLETCHER R., *Unconstrained Optimization. Practical Methods of Optimization 1*, John Wiley & Sons Ltd., 1980.

[FLE 87] FLETCHER R., *Practical Methods of Optimization*, John Wiley & Sons Ltd., 1987.

[FOG 94] FOGEL L.J., "Evolutionary programming in perspective: the top-down view" in ZURADA J.M., MARKS R.J., ROBINSON C.J. (eds), *Computational Intelligence: Imitating Life*, pp. 135–146, 1994.

[GLO 89] GLOVER F., "Tabu search – Part I", *ORSA Journal on Computing*, vol. 1, no. 3, pp. 190–206, 1989.

[GLO 90] GLOVER F., "Tabu search – Part II", *ORSA Journal on Computing*, vol. 2, no. 1, pp. 4–32, 1990.

[GOS 89] GOSS S., ARON S., DENEUBOURG J.L. *et al.*, "Self-organized Shortcuts in the Argentine Ant", *Naturwissenschaften*, vol. 76, pp. 579–581, 1989.

[HES 69] HESTENES M.R., "Multiplier and gradient methods", *Journal of Optimization Theory and Applications*, vol. 4, pp. 303–320, 1969.

[HOL 75] HOLLAND J.H., *Adaptation in Natural and Artificial System*, The University of Michigan Press, 1975.

[HU 92] HU N., "Tabu Search Method with random moves for globally optimal design", *International Journal for Numerical Methods in Engineering*, vol. 35, no. 5, pp. 1055–1070, 1992.

[KAS 95] KASPER M., HAMEYER K., KOST A., "Automated optimal design of a permanent magnet DC motor using global evolution strategy and FEM", *International Journal of Applied Electromagnetics & Mechanics*, vol. 6, pp. 367–376, 1995.

[KEN 95] KENNEDY J., EBERHART R.C., "Particle swarm optimization", *IEEE International Conference on Neural Networks Proceedings,* pp. 1942–1948, 1995.

[KIR 83] KIRKPATRICK S., GELATT C.D., VECCHI M.P., "Optimization by simulated annealing", *Science,* vol. 220, pp. 671–680, 1983.

[KOW 68] KOWALIK J., OSBORNE M.R., *Methods for Unconstrained Optimization Problems, Modern Analytic and Computational Methods in Science and Mathematics,* 1968.

[KOZ 95] KOZA J.R., *Genetic Programming,* MIT Press, 1992.

[MIC 94] MICHALEWICZ Z., *Genetic Algorithms + Data Structures = Evolution Programs,* Springer Verlag, 1994.

[NEL 65] NELDER J.A., MEAD R., "A simplex method for function minimization", *Computer Journal,* vol. 7, pp. 308–313, 1965.

[POW 65] POWELL M.J.D., "An efficient method for finding the minimum of a function of several variables without calculating derivations", *Computer Journal,* vol. 7, pp. 155–162, 1965.

[POW 69] POWELL M.J.D., *A Method for Nonlinear Constraints in Minimization Problems,* in FLETCHER, R. (ed.), *Optimization,* Academic Press, 1969.

[PRE 90] PREIS K., ZIEGLER A., "Optimal design of electromagnetic devices with Evolution Strategies", *COMPEL,* vol. 9, suppl. A, pp. 119–122, 1990.

[PRE 92] PRESS W.H., *Numerical Recipes in C: The Art of Scientific Computing,* Cambridge University Press, 1992.

[RAO 96] RAO S.S., *Engineering Optimization: Theory and Practice,* John Wiley & Sons Ltd., 1996.

[RAY 73] RAY W.H., SZEKELY J., *Process Optimization,* John Wiley & Sons Ltd., 1973.

[REC 94] RECHENBERG I., "Evolution strategy", *Computational Intelligence Imitating Life,* IEEE Press, pp. 147–159, 1994.

[ROC 73] ROCKAFFELAR R.T., "A dual approach to solving nonlinear programming problems by unconstrained optimization", *Mathematical Programming,* vol. 12, no. 6, pp. 555–562, 1973.

[SAL 98] SALUDJIAN L., COULOMB J.L., IZABELLE A., "Genetic Algorithm and Taylor development of the finite element solution for shape optimization of electromagnetic devices", *IEEE Transactions on Magnetics*, vol. 34, no. 5, pp. 2841–2844, 1998.

[SIA 14] SIARRY P., *Métaheuristiques*, Eyrolles, 2014.

[TAK 96] TAKAHASHI N., EBIHARA K., YOSHIDA K. *et al.*, "Investigation of simulating annealing method and its application to optimal design of die mold for orientation of magnetic powder", *IEEE Transactions on Magnetics*, vol. 32, no. 3, pp. 1210–1213, 1996.

[TAL 09] TALBI E.G., *Metaheuristics: From Design to Implementation*, John Wiley & Sons Ltd., 2009.

[WIL 67] WILDE D.J., Beightler C.S., *Foundations of Optimization*, Prentice Hall, 1967.

Metaheuristics for Robotics

2.1. Introduction

Nowadays, metaheuristics are used in numerous areas of engineering. This is due to the increased complexity of optimization problems and especially the high numbers of constraints that need to be respected, which make the search for optimal solutions very difficult or even unattainable in a finite time in some cases. Consequently, metaheuristics have been introduced to approximate the optimal solution as closely as possible (without any certainty that it will be reached) in a reasonable time. Robotics is one of the areas where metaheuristics are increasingly being used due to the ever more complex structures of robots; the large numbers of integrated sensors used and therefore also the large amount of information to be processed; and the environment in which they operate.

It is very difficult to define the field of robotics. In academic literature, many types of machines can be found that can be described as robots. One way to categorize them is to separate robots used only in research and robots developed for a specific need in industry or engineering:

1) *Robots used in research*: these are platforms designed to validate algorithms for trajectory planning, navigation,

perception, etc. One good example is the Turtlebot, which is a programmable platform based on ROS (Robotic Operating System) used for validating planning techniques.

2) *Robots used in engineering:* these are robots developed for a specific need. In this category, manipulative arms are the most common. Furthermore, at the time of writing, in the majority of assembly and production chains, a wide variety of tasks were carried out by manipulative arms. Surgery is also interested in the introduction of this type of robot. In this field, their use is highly beneficial to greatly increaseing the precision of the surgical gesture. Other types of robots can be included in this category such as exoskeletons, which are primarily used for supporting rehabilitation, and BigDog, developed by Boston Dynamics, which has a number of features designed for military needs.

In our study, we will more specifically focus on manipulative arms. In this chapter, we will illustrate the different ways in which metaheuristics are applied to solve the most common problems, namely trajectory planning problems and automatic control problems.

This chapter is structured in four sections. Section 2.2 gives a detailed description of the use of metaheuristics to solve trajectory planning problems. Section 2.3 provides an overview of the application of metaheuristics to solve automatic control problems. Finally, section 2.4 concludes this chapter with a brief summary.

2.2. Metaheuristics for trajectory planning problems

The purpose of the trajectory planning problem is to determine a trajectory (thus a set of positions) that will be followed by the robot in order to accomplish a particular task. Solving the problem of trajectory planning is very complex and therefore geometric modeling is often necessary. The key to its resolution resides in one's ability to reason about these types of models (representations) and to manipulate them in order to find a version from which a solution can emerge. The trajectory planning problem is strongly related to the work environment of the robot. As a matter of fact, in addition to the nature of the robot, the complexity of this problem increases with the complexity of its environment.

With regard to robot motion within a known environment, its movements can be summed up in a series of "reach the goal" tasks. However, knowledge of the environment does not facilitate knowledge of the path to be followed. Hence, the problem is divided into several stages, as shown in Figure 2.1.

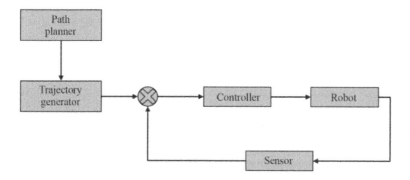

Figure 2.1. *Different stages of trajectory planning*

2.2.1. *Path planning*

As shown in Figure 2.1, the first step in trajectory planning consists of finding a path that will designate the optimal itinerary for the robot to follow. This step involves making decisions based on the task at hand and the environment of the robot. At this level, the goal is to find all the passing points that the robot must travel through in order to reach the desired final position. Each passing point corresponds to a specific configuration of the robot. The complexity at this level is strongly related to the structure of the robot (number of degrees of freedom) and also to the complexity of the working environment. Concerning manipulative arms, this step is coordinated by referring to two spaces: the joint space and the Cartesian space. The transition from one space to another can be done using the direct geometric model (DGM) or the reverse geometric model (RGM) of the robot.

2.2.1.1. *Planning within the joint space*

The joint space is characterized by joint variables. The kinematics and dynamics of the robot are often expressed inside this space. Trajectory planning, generation and tracking are directly supervised within this space by acting on the actuators of the joints, which explains the name "actuator space", and these can also be used to designate the joint space. Working in this space is tantamount to finding all the angular movements of every joint, which is obviously a very complex process. Nevertheless, this space makes it possible to take the entire structure of the robot into account, thus avoiding singular configurations, which can lead to unattainable solutions for the robot (which are located outside of its workspace). Singular configurations are often encountered by manipulating the reverse geometric pattern of the robot. A major drawback of working within this space is that it becomes very difficult to describe a robotic task with joint variables. In effect, with a robot with n degrees of freedom, the task has to be described for each of the n joints. Therefore, a proper formalization is necessary in order to achieve the specified need. Some solutions have been developed in this direction as in [YUN 96], where the authors have proposed an approach based on minimizing the movements of the robot. The reasoning is entirely done in the joint space. In addition, dynamic cinematic constraints have been taken into account.

2.2.1.2. *Planning in the Cartesian space*

The Cartesian space characterizes the evolution of the terminal organ of the robot (also called the *end effector*). In this space, the task to be performed by the end effector can be described in an accurate way. Furthermore, since the interest is in the evolution of the effector, the dimension of the search space is at most equal to 3. Therefore, it is easier to reason within this space than within a space with *n* dimensions. Here, the idea is to find the set of all the passing points of the end effector. In order to take into account the structure of the robot, some researchers have proposed expressing the kinematics and the dynamics of the robot in the Cartesian space (a solution not often used because of the complexity of computation). Others have only used the kinematics of the robot (by means of the Jacobian) to connect the two spaces. In this case, the search is carried out within the Cartesian space, taking into account the constraints imposed by the structure of the robot. An example of this approach is proposed in [YU 96], where the authors have formulated the problem in the Cartesian space. The approach makes use of all the information obtained from the workspace and makes it possible to avoid obstacles. The idea is that, starting from the base of the robot, the different segments constituting the manipulator are addressed one after the other. The end effector of the robot is also considered as a segment (assimilating it with the closest geometric shape). As a result, for each segment, evolving in 3D, its motion is transformed into 2D where path planning and obstacle avoidance are dealt with.

Working within either space has pros and cons. In addition to the usual constraints that are assumed to solve this problem, an important decision that affects the entire resolution methodology is the representation of the environment of the robot. Furthermore, the definition of the information that will be used to achieve new configurations is one of the major criteria for the solution. Therefore, there are two possible choices:

– considering the entire workspace as a source of information: in this case, this can be regarded as a global process and the methods as global methods;

– taking small parts of the workspace as a source of information: here, the workspace is divided into small regions which are successively taken into account.

With so-called global methods, a comprehensive knowledge of the robot's working environment is required. Therefore, there is no room for the unexpected. In complex environments, these methods are very expensive in terms of computational time due to the large amount of information to be processed. However, given that the environment is static, an *offline* resolution can be considered. In this way, this time constraint is solved. Another drawback of these methods is that it is difficult to integrate new constraints. For static environments where tasks are repetitive, this methodology demonstrates all of its potential.

For so-called local methods, the principle action is the breaking down of the workspace into small parts (regions) and treating them consecutively. For this technique, we can imagine online processing. Here, it is clear that the computational time is not a constraint of the problem. In addition, using this method enables new constraints to be easily integrated into the problem. These methods prove their advantages in dynamic environments.

Finding a solution for this problem can be very complicated. Hence, researchers have resorted to metaheuristics. When talking about metaheuristics as a means of resolution, we must be able, as background work, to formalize this whole problem in the form of an optimization problem. Within this context, the most important criteria are:

– minimization of the position error needed to achieve the final configuration;

– minimization of the travel time;

– minimization of energy consumption;

– minimization of velocities, accelerations and jerks.

Further criteria such as avoiding obstacles can be added. Several formulations have been proposed in the literature. Among these, we can find single-objective formulations where all criteria are grouped into a single one with weighting factors. This can be seen in [SOL 01], where the authors have proposed the objective function represented by equation 2.1:

$$F = \beta_1 f_T + \beta_2 f_I + \beta_3 f_F \qquad\qquad [2.1]$$

where β_1, β_2 and β_3 are weighting parameters. The functions f_I and f_F respectively represent the measured distance between the current position reached and the initial and final positions. The function f_T is a composition of several criteria to be optimized: velocities and accelerations in both the Cartesian and joint spaces.

In [CHE 04], the authors have used a different approach. The idea is to establish the link between two successive configurations by minimizing an objective function and taking into account constraints related to kinematics and dynamics. Equation 2.2 represents the function to be optimized:

$$F = \mu T + \frac{1-\mu}{2}[\alpha A + (1 - \alpha)B] \qquad\qquad [2.2]$$

where μ and α are weighting parameters. With this formulation, the function F reflects the cost between the initial and final configurations. In fact, the goal is to make a kind of balance between the minimization of the travel time T, torques A and energy B.

From these two illustrations, it can be seen that the formulations that can be found in the literature can range from a simple linear combination of several criteria to more complex formulations. This complexity depends essentially on the number of constraints to be considered.

Other authors have proposed multi-objective formulations. In this case, the result is a set of solutions (Pareto front). In [SOL 07], the authors worked with five criteria to be simultaneously minimized:

– minimization of the joint velocity;

– minimization of joint accelerations;

– minimization of movements (of the end effector);

– minimization of the end effector velocity;

– energy minimization.

Later, Pareto fronts are plotted in order to choose the best solutions:

– joint velocity versus Cartesian velocity;

– joint position versus Cartesian position.

In [MAR 12], the authors imbricated an optimization problem inside a control loop. In their study, they pointed out the complexity of this problem, especially the effective management of the redundancy of the robot. As a result, they defined a multi-objective optimization problem to solve the reverse kinematics problem, and also to control the joint variables. They proposed two objective functions. The first function consists of minimizing the movements of the robot, which is represented by equation 2.3:

$$F_1 = \dot{q}^T \dot{q} + \left(\frac{q-q_0}{\Delta t}\right)^T \left(\frac{q-q_0}{\Delta t}\right) \qquad [2.3]$$

where q and q_0 represent the current and initial positions of joint variables respectively, $\dot{q}$ represents the joint velocity and Δt represents the sampling time. The second function is represented by equation 2.4:

$$F_2 = X_e = \sqrt{(x_r - x_f)^2 + (y_r - y_f)^2} \qquad [2.4]$$

where X_e is the position error of the end effector (between the current position and the desired position).

In order to implement these objective functions, the authors have defined decision criteria to validate the results. By varying several parameters and plotting the Pareto front between the two functions, a set of solutions can be found and therefore the final solution can be established.

The question that arises is how a choice can be made between a single-objective function and a multi-objective function. The choice is not simple and depends on the criteria defined. Moreover, grouping several criteria with weights is not as trivial as it seems and this combination needs to be justified.

With regard to the use of Pareto fronts, these can be of interest if the defined criteria are contradictory. Therefore, with a solution curve, the right compromise can be found.

In order to take advantage of the benefits of the two planning spaces, other methods that can be described as hybrids have been developed. The main idea is to find a configuration (a position) inside one of the two spaces and to verify it in the second space (position found in the joint space to be verified in the Cartesian space or vice versa). It is clear that these methods are much more applicable when the search is local.

2.2.1.3. *Hybrid planning: joint space -> Cartesian space*

The idea of this type of technique is shown in Figure 2.2.

Figure 2.2. *Hybrid planning: joint space -> Cartesian space*

In this strategy, the first step consists of finding new configurations in the joint space. This is achieved by defining the appropriate objective functions to be minimized. Next, this joint configuration is transposed to the Cartesian space by way of the direct geometric pattern. Therefore, a new position for the end effector of the robot is obtained. The latter is verified against the preset objectives. If the result is validated, the search for a new solution continues in the joint space. In this technique, only the direct geometric model is used, which constitutes an advantage. In addition, singular configurations are automatically avoided.

The disadvantage of such methods is that it is important to correctly choose the criteria to be optimized, in order to guarantee that the solutions found are acceptable. In addition, from the user's point of view, it is easier to track the evolution of the effector than the configurations of the robot.

Several works in the literature have addressed the planning problem from this perspective. An example of this strategy is illustrated in [MAC 13]. In this work, the authors have made use of both the joint space to generate solutions and the Cartesian space to verify the non-collision of the various obstacles that may be found in the workspace. The following figure shows the approach used in this work.

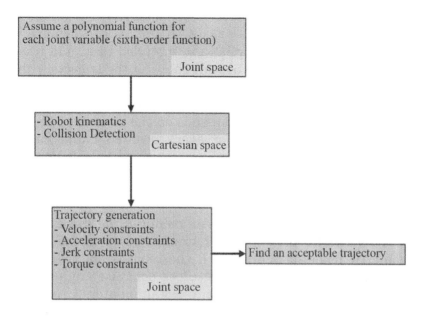

Figure 2.3. *An example of a hybrid planning strategy*

From this figure, it is clear that both spaces can be used in planning, and therefore a kind of hybrid planning is elaborated. Obviously, this example merely gives an idea of the possible use of both spaces at the same time. Depending on formalizations, further uses of both spaces can be easily imagined.

2.2.1.4. *Hybrid planning: Cartesian space -> joint space*

This technique is the opposite of the previous one, as shown in Figure 2.4.

Figure 2.4. *Hybrid planning: Cartesian space -> joint space*

With this technique, successive positions are generated for the end effector of the robot so that it can achieve its objective and thus accomplish the intended task, and it will be easier to visualize the overall shape of the trajectory that will be taken by the robot. Furthermore, the search will be done in three dimensions unlike the previous strategy where the dimension of the space depends on the number of degrees of freedom of the robot. For every position found for the end effector in the Cartesian space, we look for the corresponding joint configuration. To this end, two possible methods can be used:

– *Using the reverse geometric model of the robot*: in this case, we look for the joint configuration based on the reverse geometric model of the robot. If the robot is not redundant, shifting between the two spaces does not raise any problem. In the case of redundant manipulators, singular configurations can occur (which correspond to solutions not attainable by the robot) and thus the Jacobian matrix is not square. Several techniques have been developed to solve this problem, such as using the pseudo reverse or by adding additional constraints in order to have a square Jacobian matrix and thus be able to calculate its inverse correctly. This methodology requires complex computations that increase considerably with the number of degrees of freedom of the robot. Therefore, this solution should be used with caution. An example of this strategy is illustrated in [MAR 12].

– *Using the position found as a constraint in search of a solution*: in this case, an optimization problem is defined in the joint space with the appropriate criteria and constraints. One of the constraints of this problem is that the configuration that is found transformed into a Cartesian position must be as close as possible to the position previously found for the end effector. The advantage of this approach is that the reverse geometric model of the robot is not used, which facilitates computations and avoids singular configurations [MEN 15]. A detailed example using this approach will be presented in the next chapter.

At this level, we have only illustrated the different types of formulations of planning problems that can be encountered in the literature. The most commonly used metaheuristics are the particle swarm algorithm [HUA 08] and evolutionary algorithms [MAR 10, MAR 12].

Particle swarm algorithm

This algorithm is part of the population-based metaheuristics family. Its principle lies in the use of a population of candidate solutions in order to develop an optimal solution to a problem. Like most metaheuristics, it is inspired by the social behavior of animals that congregate in swarms, such as schools of fish and clustered bird flights. In effect, we can note in these animals relatively complex motion dynamics, whereas at the individual level, each individual possesses limited intelligence and has only local knowledge of its situation inside the swarm.

The local information and memory of each individual are used to decide about movement. Simple rules, such as staying close to other individuals, continuing in the same direction or keeping the same speed are sufficient to maintain the cohesion of the swarm, and thus allow the implementation of complex collective and adaptive behaviors.

The swarm is composed of a population of simple agents, called particles. Each particle is considered to be a probable solution to the problem, which is characterized by a position (solution vector) and a velocity. In addition, each particle owns a memory that allows it to memorize its best performance (in position and velocity), and also the best performance achieved by neighboring particles (informant).

Furthermore, each particle has a group of informants, called a neighborhood.

In the process of finding the optimal solution, each particle is influenced by three components:

– *inertia component*: the particle tends to follow its current direction of movement;

– *cognitive component*: the particle tends to move towards the best site through which it has already passed;

– *social component*: the particle tends to rely on the experience of its counterparts and thus tends to move towards the best site already reached by its neighbors.

This is shown in Figure 2.5.

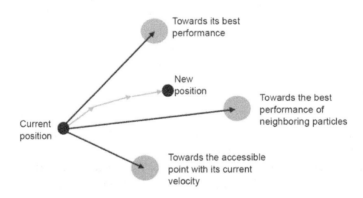

Figure 2.5. *Principle of a particle swarm algorithm*

In some formulations, particles may acquire a physical meaning. Therefore, the evolution of these particles within the swarm can be interpreted, and it will be easier to understand the resolution process. Here, the basic version of the algorithm has been described to understand its principle. However, several versions (variants) of this algorithm have been developed to accelerate its convergence and better manage the information required for particle motion.

Evolutionary algorithms

Evolutionary algorithms are techniques inspired by the evolution of living beings to solve optimization problems. Their main idea lies in that individuals that have inherited characteristics well adapted to their environment tend to live long enough to reproduce, while the weaker tend to disappear. Similar to the particle swarm algorithm, this algorithm is also population-based. Nevertheless, the individual is the main focus of interest, not the particle.

Individuals subject to evolution are possible solutions to the problem posed and the set of all these individuals constitute the population. The latter evolves over the course of successive iterations, called generations. At each generation, operators are applied to individuals, in order to create the population of the next generation. Each of these operators uses one or more individuals, called parents, to create new individuals, called children. At the end of each generation, a set of children created during the generation replaces a subset of individuals in the population.

An evolutionary algorithm involves three main operators:

– *Selection operator*: The role of the selection operator is to promote the propagation of best solutions in the population, while keeping a certain genetic diversity within the population. As a result, this operator makes it possible to choose the parents that will participate in the creation of children, and several techniques can be found, of which the following can be mentioned:

- roulette selection: its principle is to associate each individual with a probability proportional to its *fitness*, which measures the adequacy of a solution to the resolution of a problem. Following this step, we spin the roulette wheel and parents are selected. Consequently, parents exhibiting better *fitness* are more likely to be selected;

- tournament selection: with this strategy, a set of parents is randomly selected (the number of parents drawn corresponds to the size of the tournament). Then, the best individual is selected.

– *Crossover operator.* This is used when creating children. Its purpose is to exchange the genes of the parents selected to create children. This operator enables the search to be intensified within the search space, which is also associated with a *crossover probability* that represents the population rate that will be affected by this operator. Several crossover techniques have been developed such as:

- single-point crossover: the idea is to randomly generate a cutoff position for two parents and then the information is exchanged to create children. This technique can be generalized to have a two-point or multi-point crossover;

- intermediate crossover: in this technique, each gene of the created child is calculated by a weighted sum of two genes of the two selected parents.

– *Mutation operator.* Unlike the crossover operator, this operator acts on each parent individually. Its principle is to randomly draw a component of the parent individual and to replace it with a random value. Doing so allows for continued diversification in research. Several mutation techniques can be used, including:

- Gaussian mutation: in this technique, the added value to the selected gene originates from a Gaussian distribution law;

- polynomial mutation: in this technique, a polynomial distribution is used for creating children.

In addition to these three operators, a fourth operator is used with the aim of maintaining a constant population size across generations, which is called the replacement strategy. There are several techniques such as replacing all parents with created children or keeping the best parents and replacing bad ones with created children. Details about these different operators can be found in [TAL 09].

The general principle of an evolutionary algorithm is shown in Figure 2.6.

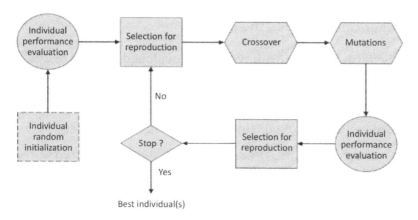

Figure 2.6. Principle of an evolutionary algorithm

2.2.2. Trajectory generation

Once the different positions are calculated, the trajectory generation aims to find the optimal path that joins these different positions. The purpose of this interpolation operation is to produce smooth curves at the position, velocity and acceleration levels. The main point is to reduce sudden and anachronistic movements that are likely to present a resonance risk that could damage the mechanical structure of the robot.

In the literature, this problem is addressed in two different ways:

– the first way is the one presented so far, namely by calculating all the crossover points and then proceeding with the smoothing operation;

– the second way is to assume at the outset that the end effector and the different joints follow particular trajectories and then to determine the coefficients that characterize each of them. In this case, with regard to Figure 2.1, the two stages of path planning and trajectory generation become a single step. It is clear that the use of this method will add further constraints to the problem.

Several techniques have been developed to ensure smooth curves; among the most widely used are splines [LIU 13], B-splines [GAS 07, GAS 10] and piecewise interpolation [TIA 04]. The simplest are the use of polynomial functions. To this end, we can consider two examples of usage:

– *using a single polynomial that passes through all the points calculated in the previous step.* This case is interesting if the number of passing points is not significant. Moreover, with a large number of passing points, it will be necessary to increase the dimension of the polynomial used, which will further complicate the calculation of different coefficients;

– *using a polynomial function between each couple of passing points.* In this case, polynomials of small dimension can be used. However, it is important to ensure the continuity of the curves at the position, velocity and acceleration levels.

Metaheuristics can also be used for this second stage. In practice, this problem can quickly become very complex because of the number of constraints to be respected. A practical example of this step will be presented later.

Once the two steps are completed, the ideal trajectory or the setpoint is generated. Therefore, the next step consists of controlling the robot in order to follow this setpoint and complete the intended task, which constitutes a problem belonging to automation control.

2.3. Metaheuristics for automatic control problems

In order to better understand automatic control problems in robotics, the concept of task function is often used. This function was introduced by Claude Samson, Bernard Espiau and Patrick le Borgne in their book *Robot Control* [SAM 91]. The purpose of this function is to translate a given robotic task into a mathematical function. This mathematical transformation is carried out directly in the sensor space, which will then enable the development of a control law and make it possible to control the robot. The principle of this formalism consists of performing a robotic task by regulating (to zero) an error function $e(q,t)$ of the configuration vector q and the time variable t.

To better understand this notion, let us consider a manipulator and assume that we wish to move its end effector (terminal organ) P according to a given trajectory $e_d(t)$, as shown in Figure 2.7.

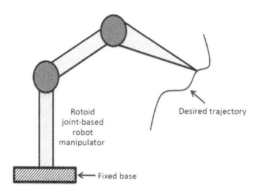

Rotoid
joint-based
robot
manipulator

Desired trajectory

Fixed base

Figure 2.7. *Trajectory outline*

If we describe by r the situation of the effector p, then a task function corresponding to this situation can be written as:

$$E(q,t) = q - e_d(t)$$

Setting $e(q, t)$ to zero makes it possible to move P according to the desired trajectory. As already illustrated, in the case of the manipulator, two workspaces can be distinguished, namely the Cartesian space and the joint space. Therefore, other types of robotic tasks described within different spaces can be specified with this formalism:

– in the joint space, a task function allowing for position regulation can be written as:

$$E(q, t) = q - q_d(t)$$

where q represents the joint position and $q_d(t)$ represents the ideal trajectory to follow in this space.

– in the Cartesian space, with the same principle and for controlling situations, we obtain:

$$E(q, t) = r(q) - r_d(t)$$

where $r(q)$ is a given parameterization of the attitude of the end effector and $r_d(t)$ represents the ideal trajectory expressed in the Cartesian space.

With this formalism of the task function, a number of properties can be derived thereof, for example the notion of the admissibility of a task. The latter consists of ensuring whether a given task is feasible or not.

Once the error is well defined, an algorithm is used to reduce it over iterations, which is the regulating process. The goal is to make the system follow the desired setpoint while ensuring velocity, accuracy and robustness. The typical response of a system is shown in Figure 2.8.

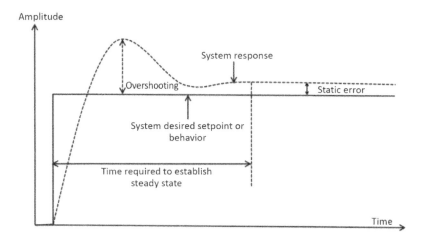

Figure 2.8. *Typical system response*

As shown in the figure, some parameters need to be verified during the regulating control:

– the rising time must be very short to ensure a quick response;

– overshooting must be minimized because excessive overshooting can lead to divergence of the response;

– in the steady or established state, the static error must be very small (if not zero).

One of the most widely used regulators in the industry is the PID regulator. This regulator is composed of three actions:

– proportional action: P;

– integral action: I.

– derived action: D.

Each of these actions has an impact on the error to be minimized. This regulator is used either for regulating in order to quickly minimize disturbances (fixed setpoint) or for tracking in order to quickly adapt to new setpoints (servo-mechanism).

The actions of the PID regulator are as follows:

1) Proportional action:

In the proportional action, the error is multiplied by a constant *Kp*. If we consider the error signal represented by *e(t)*, the output of the proportional action is represented by:

$$U(t) = Kp.e(t)$$

The bigger the *Kp*, the faster the response (reduced rising time). In addition, the static error is reduced.

2) Integral action:

As the name suggests, for the integral action, the error is integrated with an integration constant. The output of the integral action is:

$$U(t) = Ki. \int_0^t e(\tau)\, d\tau$$

The function of the integral action is to correct the static error. For higher *Ki*, the correction of the static error is increased.

3) *Derived action:*

For the derived action, the error is derived with respect to time and then multiplied by a constant *Kd*; the output of the derived action is as follows:

$$U(t) = Kd.\frac{de(t)}{dt}$$

The derived action is intended to reduce overshoots, but does not affect the static error. It should also be noted that this action is sensitive to noise.

Table 2.1 summarizes the effect of each action of the PID regulator.

Coefficient	Rising time	Stabilization time	Overshoot	Static error
Kp	Decreases	Increases	Increases	Decreases
Ki	Decreases	Increases	Increases	Cancels
Kd	-	Decreases	Decreases	-

Table 2.1. *Effects of the actions of the PID regulator*

The PID regulator is used in several areas of the industry. This is due to its efficiency and ease of implementation. The PID regulator can be applied to any type of system (linear, nonlinear) and with or without knowledge of these latter (white box or black box). In practice and for large numbers of systems, the Ziegler Nichols technique is used to adjust the parameters of the regulator (various gains). Nevertheless, due to the complexity and dynamics of some systems (such as exoskeletons) and also to make the use of this regulator more generic, researchers continue to work on the PID regulator and propose solutions with the aim that it will become adaptable to any type of system. This is interesting, especially if no knowledge is available about the system to be regulated. One of the ideas is to use metaheuristics to find the parameters of the algorithm [KIM 08, ALF 11, BEL 17]. In [BEL 17], the authors adapted the use of a PSO algorithm to find gains *kp*, *Ki* and *Kd*. By defining the correct objective function and adjusting the use and displacements of the different particles, they were able to stabilize the control signal and properly control the system even without any knowledge of the latter. The details of this technique are presented in Chapter 5.

2.4. Conclusion

In this chapter, a general overview of the trajectory planning of manipulative arms was presented. The various steps taken into account to address this problem and the use of metaheuristics for the resolution were illustrated. The trajectory planning problem still remains a highly topical research subject. In fact, researchers are increasingly working on improving current solutions to accuracy, real-time performance and adaptability to different systems.

2.5. Bibliography

[ALF 11] ALFI A., MODARES H., "System identification and control using adaptive particle swarm optimization", *Applied Mathematical Modelling,* vol. 35, no. 3, pp. 1210–1221, 2011.

[BEL 17] BELKADI A., OULHADJ H., TOUATI Y. *et al.,* "On the robust PID adaptive controller for exoskeletons: A particle swarm optimization-based approach", *Applied Soft Computing,* vol. 60, pp. 87–100, 2017.

[CHE 04] CHETTIBI T., LEHTIHET H.E., HADDAD M. *et al.,* "Minimum cost trajectory planning for industrial robots", *European Journal of Mechanics A: Solids,* vol. 23, pp. 703–715, 2004.

[GAS 07] GASPARETTO A., ZANOTTO V., "A new method for smooth trajectory planning of robot manipulators", *Mechanism and Machine Theory,* vol. 42, pp. 455–471, 2007.

[GAS 10] GASPARETTO A., ZANOTTO V., "Optimal trajectory planning for industrial robots", *Advances in Engineering Software,* vol. 41, pp. 548–556, 2010.

[HUA 08] HUANG P., LIU G., YUAN J., XU Y., "Multi-objective optimal trajectory planning of space robot using particle swarm optimization", *5th International Composium on Neural Networks,* Beijing, China, September 24–28, 2008.

[KIM 08] KIM T.H., MARUTA I., SUGIE T., "Robust PID controller tuning based on the constrained particle swarm optimization", *Automatica*, vol. 44, no. 4, pp. 1104–1110, 2008.

[LIU 13] LIU H., LAI X., WU W., "Time-optimal and jerk continuous trajectory planning for robot manipulators with kinematic constraints", *Robotics and Computer-Integrated Manufacturing*, vol. 29, pp. 309–317, 2013.

[MAC 13] MACHMUDAH A., PARMAN S., ZAINUDDIN A. *et al.*, "Polynomial joint angle arm robot motion planning in complex geometric obstacles", *Applied Soft Computing*, vol. 13, pp. 1099–1109, 2013.

[MAR 10] MARIA DA GRAÇA M., TENREIRO MACHADO J.A., AZEVEDO-PERDICOULIS T.-P., "An evolutionary approach for the motion planning of redundant and hyper-redundant manipulators", *Nonlinear Dynamics,* vol. 60, pp. 115–129, 2010.

[MAR 12] MARIA DA GRAÇA M., TENREIRO MACHADO J.A., AZEVEDO-PERDICOULIS T.-P., "A multi-objective approach for the motion planning of redundant manipulators", *Applied Soft Computing*, vol. 12, pp. 589–599, 2012.

[MEN 15] MENASRI R., NAKIB A., DAACHI B. *et al.*, "A trajectory planning of redundant manipulators based on bilevel optimization", *Applied Mathematics and Computation*, vol. 250, pp. 934–947, 2015.

[SAM 91] SAMSON C., LE BORGNE M., ESPIAU B., *Robot Control: The Task Function Approach*, Clarendon Press, 1991.

[SOL 01] SOLTEIRO PIRES E.J., TENREIRO MACHADO J.A., DE MOURA OLIVEIRA P.B., "An evolutionary approach to robot structure and trajectory optimization", *10th International Conference on Advanced Robotics 2001*, Budapest, Hungary, August 2001.

[SOL 07] SOLTEIRO PIRES E.J., DE MOURA OLIVEIRA P.B., TENEIRO MACHADO J.A., "Manipulator trajectory planning using a MOEA", *Applied Soft Computing*, vol. 7, pp. 659–667, 2007.

[TAL 09] TALBI E.G., *Metaheuristics: From Design to Implementation*, John Wiley & Sons, 2009.

[TIA 04] TIAN L., COLLINS C., "An effective robot trajectory planning method using a genetic algorithm", *Mechatronics*, vol. 14, pp. 455–470, 2004.

[YU 96] YU J.S., MULLER P.C., "An on-line cartesian space obstacle avoidance scheme for robot arms", *Mathematics and Computers in Simulation*, vol. 41, pp. 627–637, 1996.

[YUN 96] YUN W.M., XI Y.G., "Optimum motion planning in joint space for robots using genetic algorithms", *Robotics and Autonomous Systems*, vol. 18, pp. 373–393, 1996.

Metaheuristics for Constrained and Unconstrained Trajectory Planning

3.1. Introduction

In this chapter, a trajectory planning method will be presented. With regard to the different steps shown in Figure 2.1 of Chapter 2, it concerns the *path planning* section, which is defined by a set of positions through which the robot should pass. In this approach, a new strategy is developed based on the bilevel optimization technique. With regard to the different classifications presented in the previous chapter, the hybrid planning class covers two complementary spaces: the Cartesian space and the joint space.

The main idea is to adapt the planning problem to the class of the bilevel optimization problem by defining the appropriate criteria. In this case, the focus will be on redundant manipulative arms, the redundancy being used to avoid obstacles as well as for the management of robot singularities. For the resolution method, a metaheuristic based on genetic algorithms will be used.

This chapter is composed of eight sections. The technique adopted for avoiding obstacles is described in section 3.2. Section 3.3 provides a general overview of bilevel optimization problems. The proposed formulation is described in section 3.4. The solving algorithm is presented in section 3.5. The simulation results obtained with the model of the Neuromate robot are presented in section 3.6. Finally, a conclusion and a list of bibliographical references are given in sections 3.7 and 3.8 respectively.

3.2. Obstacle avoidance

When the robot moves about within its environment, it is important to detect the presence of obstacles in its path and above all to avoid them. Consequently, two questions arise:

– How does the robot perceive these obstacles?

– How will it be able to avoid collisions with these obstacles?

The answer to the first question depends heavily on the electronic equipment embedded in the robot. For example, if the robot is equipped with sensors and/or cameras, the perception of obstacles becomes an analysis and data processing (signals, images) problem. In our study, we will consider the case in which the robot is devoid of sensors. Therefore, modeling the obstacles is necessary. Obviously, taking into account the actual form of obstacles is more interesting; however, this will have a considerable impact on the obstacle avoidance technique applied, especially in terms of computational effort. Hence, making use of hypersurfaces (circles, spheres, ellipses, etc.) is often advocated in the literature.

Doing so will facilitate the measurement of the distance between the robot and the new form of obstacles. On the contrary, the free workspace of the robot will be reduced. Nonetheless, this solution is adopted because it is better suited to the technique for obstacle avoidance that will be presented later. Therefore, starting from any original form of the obstacle, it is enveloped with the hypersurface of minimal radius. Figure 3.1 provides an illustrative example of this process.

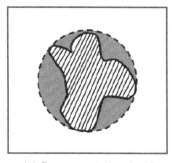

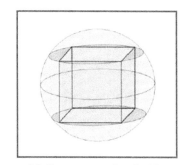

(a) Representation in 2D   *(b) Representation in 3D*

Figure 3.1. *Obstacle modeling. For a color version of this figure, see www.iste.co.uk/oulhadj/metaheuristics.zip*

In this way, the obstacle will be surrounded by a circle of minimal radius in a 2D space and by a sphere in a 3D space.

With regard to the second question, avoiding the obstacle, the technique described hereafter is developed. This technique is basic, but it has the advantage of being adaptive. It is also based on the assumption that *offline* processing will be used in cases where the positions of the various obstacles are known in advance.

Several obstacle avoidance techniques have been proposed in the literature [POU 91, LEB 06, DAA 12, PER 02]. Each one of them can be distinguished by the chosen shape of the robot, that of the obstacles and the distance measured between the two. In our study, control points are defined to measure this distance. These are the result of the intersection of the normal passing through the central point of each obstacle and the line formed by the two centers of two successive joints, as shown in Figure 3.2.

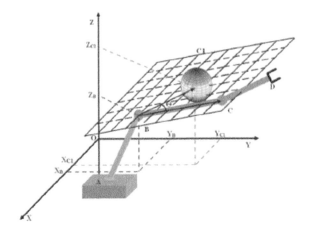

Figure 3.2. *Plane used to measure distances. For a color version of this figure, see www.iste.co.uk/oulhadj/metaheuristics.zip*

For every obstacle and in relation to each robot arm, the measurement is carried out on the plane defined by the center of the obstacle and the two centers of two successive joints. Therefore, in Figure 3.2, the plane is formed by points *B*, *C* and *C1*, respectively forming the two centers of the two joints and the center of the obstacle. In order to better understand this approach, a planar robot with three degrees of freedom and an obstacle in the form of a disk are considered, as shown in Figure 3.3.

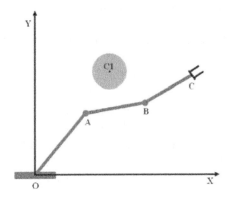

Figure 3.3. *Planar robot with an obstacle*

This robot is composed of three arms: *OA*, *AB* and *BC*. This technique will be illustrated for the arm *AB*, knowing that the final formulation and implementation will be applied to each arm and every obstacle. With such a configuration for the robot and the obstacle, three separate cases may emerge, as shown in Figure 3.4.

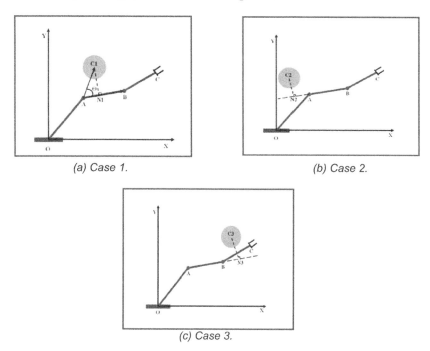

(a) Case 1.   (b) Case 2.

(c) Case 3.

Figure 3.4. *Illustrated example of obstacle detection*

In the first case, shown in Figure 3.4(a), the intersection point of the normal passing through the center of the obstacle (point *C1*) belongs to the line formed by the two points *A* and *B*. Therefore, we need to make sure that the distance /*N1C1*/ is greater than the radius of the obstacle. In the other two cases, presented in Figure 3.4(b) and (c), the intersection point of the normal with the line passing through *A* and *B* does not belong to the segment delimited by *A* and *B*. As a result, it is not necessary to verify whether or not the distance $/N1C1/$ is greater than the radius of the obstacle.

In order to verify whether point $N1$ belongs to segment AB, the dot product of the two vectors AB and $AC1$ is calculated. Next, we decide whether $N1$ belongs to segment AB by verifying the following two assumptions:

$$|AC1|.cos(\theta) \leq |AB|$$

with: $-\frac{\pi}{2} \leq \theta \leq \frac{\pi}{2}$

where $/AC1/$ and $/AB/$ represent the norms of both vectors $\overrightarrow{AB}$ and $\overrightarrow{AC}$ respectively. The consequence of such an approach is that the number of control points is variable, since it depends on the position of each obstacle in relation to each arm. As a result, at every iteration and for each arm, we can have two or three control points.

3.3. Bilevel optimization problem

Bilevel optimization problems can be included in hierarchical optimization problems. The latter form a class of problems where a decision-making process represents a decisive step in search of solutions. As the name suggests, in bilevel optimization problems, two levels (tiers) of decisions are taken into account. Each of them has its own objective function and constraints. Therefore, a subset of decision variables is managed by the first level and the rest of the variables are managed by the second level. During iterations, an objective function specific to each level is optimized by taking into account some of the decisions made at the other level. This bilevel optimization process can be formulated as follows:

$$min_x F(x,y)$$

with: $G(x,y) \leq 0$

$$min_y f(x, y)$$

with: $g(x, y) \leq 0$

where $x \in R^{n1}$ and $y \in R^{n2}$ are the variables controlled by the first and second levels respectively. $F, f : R^n \to R, n = n1 + n2$. $G(x, y)$ and $g(x, y)$ represent the constraints of inequality.

3.4. Formulation of the trajectory planning problem

As mentioned earlier, the proposed formulation concerns the class of bilevel optimization problems. Each of the two levels corresponds to one of the planning spaces for the manipulator arms. Therefore, the first level will treat the Cartesian space (end effector space) and the second level will treat the joint space (actuator space).

At the first level, we look for new positions for the end effector (the terminal organ of the robot) while staying away from the various obstacles. As soon as a new position is found, it will be transmitted to the second level, which will in turn find the best configuration (of joint variables) by making use of the redundancy of the robot. The adopted formulation is as follows:

$$min_x F(X, \theta) = \alpha. F1(X) + \beta. (X - Xc) + \gamma. F2(\theta) \qquad [3.1]$$

Under the constraints:

$$G1(X) \leq 0, G2(X) \leq 0$$

$$min_\theta L(\theta) = \delta. F3(\theta) + \zeta. F4(\theta) \qquad [3.2]$$

Under the constraints:

$$\begin{cases} g1(\theta) \leq 0, g2(\theta) \leq 0 \\ \quad H(X, \theta) = 0 \end{cases}$$

with:

$$\alpha + \beta - \gamma = 1 \text{ and } \delta - \zeta = 1; \alpha \in [0,1], \beta \in [0,1], \gamma \in [0,1], \delta \in [0,1], \zeta \in [0,1];$$

$$\alpha > \beta \text{ and } \alpha > \gamma$$

In this formulation, the parameter α is the most important. We have to make sure that it is above both parameters β and γ. With this choice, more weight is given to the function $F1(X)$, in order to strengthen our chances of reaching the final position. The different criteria and constraints are described in sections 3.4.1 and 3.4.2.

3.4.1. *Objective functions*

In the proposed formulation, two objective functions, defined respectively by equations [3.1] and [3.2], are taken into account. Equation [3.1] represents the first-level objective function. It is composed of three criteria. As mentioned above, the goal of this level is to enable the end effector to reach the desired final position, while keeping the control points away from the various obstacles. For this level, the control points are only the centers of each joint.

The first criterion is described by the function $F1(X)$; it represents the position error between the current and final positions for the end effector:

$$F1(X) = \sqrt{(x - xf)^2 + (y - yf)^2} \qquad [3.3]$$

where $X = (x,y)$ represents the current position of the end effector and (xf,yf) is the final position to be reached.

The second term of the objective function is $(X\text{-}Xc)$. The latter is used to take into account the error found by both levels for the same position of the end effector. The value of Xc is found by the second level, taking into account all of its constraints. Since this term is an indicator of the degree of satisfaction of constraints, it will make it possible to minimize over the generations the degree of dissatisfaction of the constraints taken into account at the second level.

The last term of equation [3.1] is represented by the function $F2(\theta)$. The purpose of this term is to keep the control points (the center of the joints in this case) away from the various obstacles. It is expressed as follows:

$$F2(\theta) = \sum_{i=1}^{N} \sum_{j=1}^{M} d(\theta)\{PC_i, PC_j\} \qquad [3.4]$$

where $d(\theta)\{PC_i, PC_j\}$ is the Euclidian distance between the control point PC_i and the center of each joint C_j, N is the total number of control points and M is the number of obstacles. Without the integration of this criterion, the first level will attempt to minimize its objective function without taking into account the collision with obstacles. Collisions will then occur, and it will be more difficult for the second level to find an admissible solution that meets all the constraints, the value of θ being returned by the second level.

Equation [3.2] represents the objective function of the second level, which includes two criteria. The goal of this level is to find the best configuration for each of the positions transmitted by the first level. The first criterion is represented by the function $F3(\theta)$ that is used to maximize the manipulability of the robot. Its expression can be written as:

$$F3(\theta) = \sqrt{|det\{J(\theta).J^T(\theta)\}|} \qquad [3.5]$$

where J is the Jacobian of the robot and J^T is its transpose. The Jacobian matrix is obtained by a differentiation of the direct geometric model of the robot. This matrix defines the relationship of velocities existing between the task space and the joint space, as shown in equation [3.6]:

$$\dot{X} = J(\theta).\dot{\theta} \qquad\qquad\qquad [3.6]$$

where $\dot{X}$ and $\dot{\theta}$ are the respective velocities in the task space and the joint space. Given the hypothesis of a redundant robot, this matrix is not square. However, with the proposed formulation, it is not necessary to invert it. Manipulability is considered to be one of the indices of robot performance [KUC 06]. Maximizing this variable will mean that less effort has to be applied to move the robot. Therefore, the indirectly applied torque is minimized. On the contrary, manipulability makes it possible to obtain an approximation measure of the robot with its singular configurations [KUC 06, TSA 90]. Consequently, working with maximum manipulability ensures that we avoid these configurations.

The second criterion is represented by the function $F4(\theta)$. This function is used to minimize the variation of joint variables, in order to obtain small movements. Its expression can be written as:

$$F4(\theta) = \frac{1}{2}.\sum_{i=1}^{K} q_i^2(\theta) \qquad\qquad [3.7]$$

where q_i represents the joint variables and K represents their total number.

3.4.2. Constraints

As with objective functions, each level has its constraints. For the first level, they are represented by $G1(X)$ and $G2(X)$. The purpose of the constraint $G1(X)$ is to ensure that the end effector does not collide with the various obstacles. The objective of $G2(X)$ is to minimize the movement of the end effector. Its expression can be written as:

$$G2(X) = |X(i+1) - X(i)| \leq R$$

where $X(i+1)$ is the position found for the effector at the stage $(i+1)$ and $X(i)$ is its position at the stage (i). The choice of the value of R is very important. Furthermore, the latter delimits the search space at each stage for the first level. In this way, a new position is sought for at every iteration for the end effector inside a parallelepiped.

For the second level, the constraints are represented by $g1(\theta)$, $g2(\theta)$ and $H(X,\theta)$. Constraint $g1(\theta)$ represents the lower and upper bounds of the various joint variables. Constraint $g2(\theta)$ is used for obstacle avoidance, according to the approach described in section 3.2. The equality constraint represents $H(X,\theta)$, the direct geometric model of the robot that can be calculated with the Denavit–Hartenberg convention [SHU 13]. This model represents the existing relationship between the coordinates of the end effector and the joint variables:

$$X = F(\theta) \text{ and } H(X,\theta) = X - F(\theta)$$

The idea in this formulation is to guide the search for new solutions at the first level and then refine and validate these solutions at the second level. At the first level, the search is carried out in such a way as to reach the desired final position while trying to keep the structure of the robot as far as possible away from obstacles. On the contrary, at the second level, the solution found guarantees us obstacle avoidance. The optimality of the final solution is thus ensured by both levels at the same time.

3.5. Resolution with a bigenetic algorithm

Bilevel optimization problems are appropriate models for a wide range of industrial processes. Nonetheless, their use is very limited. This is due to the lack of effective algorithms adapted to this kind of formulation. In fact, bilevel optimization problems are categorized as NP-complete problems [CAL 08], which has oriented a large amount of research in this direction in order to try to develop and/or adapt processing algorithms for this type of formulation. The result is that many techniques have been developed [JIA 13, ODU 02, HEJ 02]. The latter can be divided into two main categories:

– techniques based on the transformation of the bilevel problem into a single-level problem using the Karush–Kuhn–Tucker method [JIA 13, LV 07];

– direct resolution techniques without any transformation [ODU 02, LI 06].

The question then is whether or not it is more advantageous to transform the bilevel problem into a single-tier problem. The choice will depend on the formulations being used, their complexity and above all whether or not the problem addressed can be transformed.

For each of the two categories, numerous algorithms have been developed. Each of them deals with a particular form of the problem posed (depending on the objective function, the nature of the constraints, etc.). Therefore, a variety of algorithms can be found in the literature (particle swarm optimization [JIA 13], use of penalty functions [WAN 11], evolutionary algorithms [ODU 02, HEJ 02], etc.).

In this study, a metaheuristic making use of genetic algorithms is implemented. This choice was made because many studies based on genetic algorithms have proven their effectiveness. A genetic algorithm is therefore assigned to every processing level. The execution takes place by sequentially alternating both levels. The general bigenetic algorithm is described in Figure 3.5.

In the formulation described in section 3.4, the decision variables to be optimized at the first level represent the position of the end effector inside the Cartesian space (its coordinates). For the second level, the decision variables are the joint variables.

At the beginning of the execution, the entire population of the first level is initialized at the same point, which represents the initial position of the robot. The population is then evaluated and the operators of the genetic algorithm are applied (selection, crossover and mutation). At each generation, the first level sends its result to the second level, which starts its execution after initialization of its population with the configurations obtained at the end of its previous execution. Next, the first level waits for the result produced by the second level before resuming its execution. The two levels are thus alternated sequentially until the end of the bigenetic algorithm.

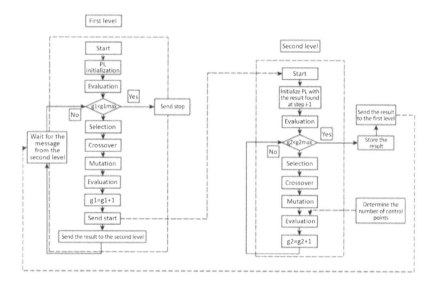

Figure 3.5. *Description of the bigenetic algorithm*

The second level, after receiving the data from the first level, begins its execution by initializing its population with the result found in the previous stage. This procedure is necessary for the function $F4(\theta)$. The aim of the latter is to minimize variations in joint variables between the previous and the new solution to be found, which also makes it possible to accelerate the convergence of the resolution algorithm.

Once the second-level population is initialized, the operators of the genetic algorithm are applied during *g2max* generations, which correspond to the highest number of generations for this level. At the end of *g2max* generations, the second level suspends its execution, saves the result found and sends it to the first level. It then starts waiting for data originating from the first level. The time and complexity of the second level depends on the number and position of the various obstacles. Furthermore, high numbers of obstacles increase the number of constraints and thus the execution time.

At the highest value of generations *g1max*, the first level sends a "STOP" message to the second level and thus signals the end of the execution of the bigenetic algorithm. As shown in Figure 3.5, an additional step is to determine the number of control points. It should be remembered that these are used to ensure that collisions with different obstacles are avoided.

At every first-level generation, *g2max* generations are produced at the second level. The total number of generations for both levels is therefore the product of *g1max* and *g2max*.

3.6. Simulation with the model of the Neuromate robot

To evaluate the developed method, the Neuromate robot is used. This assistance robot improves the ergonomics and accuracy of surgical procedures at the head level, as in the treatment of hydrocephalus. Planning a trajectory for this robot consists of bringing it back from any configuration to the one where the end effector will be positioned at a specific location above the patient's head. More details about using this robot can be found in [REN 19]. Figure 3.6 gives an overview of this robot.

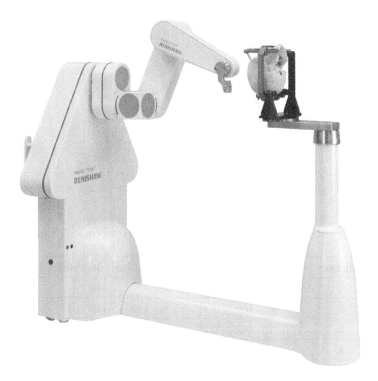

Figure 3.6. *Neuromate robot. The Neuromate robot has five degrees of freedom. All of the joints are rotating. The geometric model of this robot is calculated using the Denavit–Hartenberg convention [SHU 13]. Its kinematic model is directly obtained by differentiation of the geometric model (with the authorization of Renishaw plc). For a color version of this figure, see www.iste.co.uk/oulhadj/metaheuristics.zip*

3.6.1. *Geometric model of the Neuromate robot*

The Neuromate robot possesses a conventional kinematic structure based on five pivoting joints. The geometric configuration of the robot is shown in Figure 3.7.

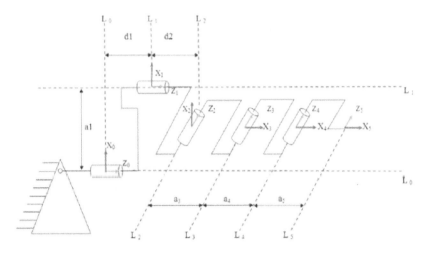

Figure 3.7. *Geometric configuration of the robot. For a color version of this figure, see www.iste.co.uk/oulhadj/metaheuristics.zip*

The limits of the joints of the robot are given in Table 3.1.

Joint no.	Min. (degrees)	Max. (degrees)
1	−180	180
2	−180	180
3	−90	90
4	−90	90
5	−90	90

Table 3.1. *Limits of the robot joints*

The Denavit–Hartenberg convention is used to calculate the coordinates of the robot end effector within a frame of reference linked to the base of the robot (fixed reference). With this convention, a relative frame of reference is assigned to each joint and the geometric parameters of the robot are determined according to Table 3.2.

Body	a_i	α_i	d_i	θ_i	ϕ_i
1	a_1	0	d_1	q_1	0
2	0	$\dfrac{\pi}{2}$	d_2	q_2	0
3	a_3	0	0	q_3	0
4	a_4	0	0	q_4	0
5	a_5	0	0	q_5	0

Table 3.2. *Geometric parameters*

The parameters (a_i, α_i, d_i, θ_i, ϕ_i), called geometric parameters, correspond to the following information:

– ϕ_i: joint type (0: rotoid and 1: prismatic);

– α_i: angle between $Z(i$–$1)$ and $Z(i)$ around $X(i)$;

– a_{i-1}: distance between $Z(i$–$1)$ and $Z(i)$ along $X(i)$;

– θ_i: angle between $X(i$–$1)$ and $X(i)$ along $Z(i$–$1)$;

– d_i: distance between $X(i$–$1)$ and $X(i)$ along $Z(i$–$1)$.

Assuming that $\cos(\theta_i) = C_i$, $\sin(\theta_i) = S_i$, $\cos(\alpha_i) = C\alpha_i$ and $\sin(\alpha_i) = S\alpha_i$, the general shape of the shift matrix between the frame of reference $R(i$–$1)$ and reference $R(i)$ is as follows:

$$T_i^{i-1} = \begin{pmatrix} C_i & -S_iC\alpha_i & S_iS\alpha_i & a_iC_i \\ S_i & C_iC\alpha_i & -C_iS\alpha_i & a_iS_i \\ 0 & S\alpha_i & C\alpha_i & d_i \\ 0 & 0 & 0 & 1 \end{pmatrix}$$

Transformation matrices can be written as:

$$T_1^0 = \begin{pmatrix} C_1 & -S_1 & 0 & a_1C_1 \\ S_1 & C_1 & 0 & a_1S_1 \\ 0 & 0 & 1 & d_1 \\ 0 & 0 & 0 & 1 \end{pmatrix} \qquad T_2^1 = \begin{pmatrix} C_2 & 0 & S_2 & 0 \\ S_2 & 0 & -C_2 & 0 \\ 0 & 1 & 0 & d_2 \\ 0 & 0 & 0 & 1 \end{pmatrix}$$

$$T_3^2 = \begin{pmatrix} C_3 & -S_3 & 0 & a_3C_3 \\ S_3 & C_3 & 0 & a_3S_3 \\ 0 & 0 & 1 & 0 \\ 0 & 0 & 0 & 1 \end{pmatrix} \qquad T_4^3 = \begin{pmatrix} C_4 & -S_4 & 0 & a_4C_4 \\ S_4 & C_4 & 0 & a_4S_4 \\ 0 & 0 & 0 & 0 \\ 0 & 0 & 0 & 1 \end{pmatrix}$$

$$T_5^4 = \begin{pmatrix} C_5 & -S_5 & 0 & a_5C_5 \\ S_5 & C_5 & 0 & a_5S_5 \\ 0 & 0 & 1 & 0 \\ 0 & 0 & 0 & 1 \end{pmatrix}$$

The direct geometric model of the robot is obtained by multiplying all these matrices. Therefore, the coordinates of the end effector are obtained in the frame of reference R_0 by calculating the product $T_5^0 = T_1^0 . T_2^1 . T_3^2 . T_4^3 . T_5^4$ called the global homogeneous matrix. To perform these computations, the Maple software can be used. The elements of matrix T_5^0 (after simplification) are:

$$T_5^0 = \begin{pmatrix} C_{12}C_{345} & -C_{12}S_{345} & S_{12} & a_5C_{12}C_{345} + a_4C_{12}C_{34} + a_3C_{12}C_3 + a_1C_1 \\ -S_{12}C_{345} & -S_{12}S_{345} & -C_{12} & a_5S_{12}C_{345} + a_4S_{12}C_{34} + a_3S_{12}C_3 + a_1S_1 \\ S_{345} & C_{345} & 0 & a_5S_{345} + a_4S_{34} + a_3S_3 + d_1 + d_2 \\ 0 & 0 & 0 & 1 \end{pmatrix}$$

The position of the end effector is given by the following matrix:

$$\begin{pmatrix} X = a_5C_{12}C_{345} + a_4C_{12}C_{34} + a_3C_{12}C_3 + a_1C_1 \\ Y = a_5S_{12}C_{345} + a_4S_{12}C_{34} + a_3S_{12}C_3 + a_1S_1 \\ Z = a_5S_{345} + a_4S_{34} + a_3S_3 + d_1 + d_2 \end{pmatrix}$$

3.6.2. *Kinematic model of the Neuromate robot*

The kinematic model of the robot describes the relationship between the velocity of the end effector $\dot{X}$ and the velocity of the joints $\dot{q}$, which is defined by:

$$\dot{X} = J.\dot{q}$$

The variable J is the Jacobi matrix, which is defined by:

$$J = \begin{pmatrix} \dfrac{\partial X}{\partial q1} & \dfrac{\partial X}{\partial q2} & \dfrac{\partial X}{\partial q3} & \dfrac{\partial X}{\partial q4} & \dfrac{\partial X}{\partial q5} \\ \dfrac{\partial Y}{\partial q1} & \dfrac{\partial Y}{\partial q2} & \dfrac{\partial Y}{\partial q3} & \dfrac{\partial Y}{\partial q4} & \dfrac{\partial Y}{\partial q5} \\ \dfrac{\partial Z}{\partial q1} & \dfrac{\partial Z}{\partial q2} & \dfrac{\partial Z}{\partial q3} & \dfrac{\partial Z}{\partial q4} & \dfrac{\partial Z}{\partial q4} \end{pmatrix}$$

with:

$$J_{11} = \frac{\partial X}{\partial q1} = -a_5 S_{12} C_{345} - a_4 S_{12} C_{34} - a_3 C_3 S_{12} - a_1 S_1$$

$$J_{12} = \frac{\partial X}{\partial q2} = -a_5 S_{12} C_{345} - a_4 S_{12} C_{34} - a_3 C_3 S_{12}$$

$$J_{13} = \frac{\partial X}{\partial q3} = -a_5 C_{12} S_{345} - a_4 C_{12} S_{34} - a_3 S_3 C_{12}$$

$$J_{14} = \frac{\partial X}{\partial q4} = -a_5 C_{12} S_{345} - a_4 C_{12} S_{34}$$

$$J_{15} = \frac{\partial X}{\partial q5} = -a_5 C_{12} S_{345}$$

$$J_{21} = \frac{\partial Y}{\partial q1} = a_5 C_{12} C_{345} + a_4 C_{12} C_{34} + a_3 C_3 C_{12} + a_1 C_1$$

$$J_{22} = \frac{\partial Y}{\partial q2} = a_5 C_{12} C_{345} + a_4 C_{12} C_{34} + a_3 C_3 C_{12}$$

$$J_{23} = \frac{\partial Y}{\partial q3} = -a_5 S_{12} S_{345} - a_4 S_{12} S_{34} - a_3 S_3 S_{12}$$

$$J_{24} = \frac{\partial Y}{\partial q4} = -a_5 S_{12} S_{345} - a_4 S_{12} S_{34}$$

$$J_{25} = \frac{\partial Y}{\partial q5} = -a_5 S_{12} S_{345}$$

$$J_{31} = \frac{\partial Z}{\partial q1} = 0$$

$$J_{32} = \frac{\partial Z}{\partial q2} = 0$$

$$J_{33} = \frac{\partial Z}{\partial q3} = a_5 C_{345} + a_4 C_{34} - a_3 S_3$$

$$J_{34} = \frac{\partial Z}{\partial q4} = a_5 C_{345} + a_4 C_{34}$$

$$J_{35} = \frac{\partial Z}{\partial q5} = a_5 C_{345}$$

3.6.3. *Simulation results*

In addition to the physical characteristics of the robot previously described, we consider the initial position of the end effector [1.1727 cm, −6.3085 cm, −0.75 cm] and the final position [5.5 cm, 1.5 cm, 0.8 cm] to be reached. For obstacle avoidance, totaling a number of 15 obstacles, all with the same radius of 0.4 cm, their positions within the robot workspace are shown in Table 3.3.

Positions	S_1	S_2	S_3	S_4	S_5	S_6	S_7	S_8	S_9	S_{10}	S_{11}	S_{12}	S_{13}	S_{14}	S_{15}
X(cm)	1	0.5	1.5	2	2	2	3	2.5	3.5	4.5	4.5	4.5	4	3	3.5
Y(cm)	−4	−4	−4	−3	−1	−2	0	0	0	1.5	2	2.5	2	2	2
Z(cm)	−0.5	−0.5	−0.5	−1.2	−1.2	−1.2	0	0	0	1	1	1	0	0	0

Table 3.3. *Position of obstacles in the robot workspace*

The first-level chromosome is composed of three genes, which correspond to the positions of the end effector in the 3D Cartesian space. The second-level chromosome is composed of five genes that represent joint variables, as shown in Figure 3.8.

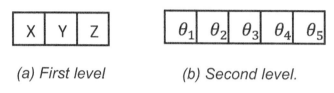

(a) First level   *(b) Second level.*

Figure 3.8. *Chromosomes of the algorithm*

With this formulation, the solutions found depend on the choice made for weighting parameters. This choice is therefore decisive. For the following tests, the parameters are set to give more importance to the first criterion corresponding to the position error, which is defined by equation 3.1. We take $\alpha = 0.4$, $\beta = 0.3$, $\gamma = -0.3$ for the first level. For the second level, greater importance is given to variations in joint variables, in accordance with equation 3.2. We thus have $\delta = -0.3$, $\zeta = 0.6$. This relevant choice is appropriate for the validation of the algorithm and the proposed formulation. For the two genetic algorithms implemented, their parameters are presented in Table 3.4.

Parameters	First level	Second level
Population size	60	70
Number of generations	20	60
Mutation rate	0.2	0.3
Crossover probability	0.6	0.6
Tournament size	4	4

Table 3.4. *Algorithm parameters*

In Table 3.4, only the number of generations and the population size are adjusted during the tests. Regarding the other parameters, the default values used in the literature are assumed. Given that the algorithm uses probabilistic operators, it is necessary to restart it several times in order to objectively validate the results of the tests. Therefore, 50 executions are taken into account. The simulation results are shown in Figures 3.9–3.16.

Figure 3.9(a) and (b) present the evolution of the best individual for the first level. This figure shows the influence of the operators of the genetic algorithm. In effect, the results clearly show the diversification due to the mutation operator and the intensification due to the crossover operator, which reinforces the choice made for the weighting parameters summarized in Table 3.4.

In Figure 3.9(b), it can be noted that the value of the objective function increases systematically before stabilizing during the last iterations, thus representing convergence. It can also be seen that the standard deviation is small at the beginning and at convergence, whereas it is more significant during intermediate iterations. At the beginning of the execution, the entire population is initialized at the same point. Theoretically, we should have zero standard deviation. However, the results show a small standard deviation due to the value of the second member of the objective function $(X–X_c)$, which is not zero. At convergence, the decrease in the standard deviation can be explained by solutions gradually grouping around the final position, guided by the data sent back by the second level. Figure 3.10(a) and (b) shows the same result at the second level. The results are shown in Figure 3.10(a) and (b), and the same conclusions about the first level can be drawn about the second level, confirming the correct choice of parameters for the two genetic algorithms implemented.

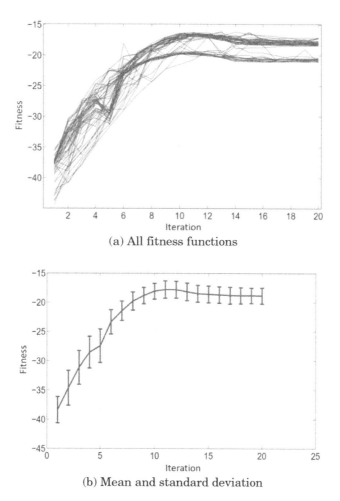

(a) All fitness functions

(b) Mean and standard deviation

Figure 3.9. *Evolution of the best individual in the first level*

Figure 3.10(b) shows the curve of mean fitness over the iterations. We recall that in the second level, the variation in joint variables is minimized while maximizing the manipulability of the robot. Theoretically, we should have an upward curve. Nevertheless, a part of this curve decreases. This is the result of the choice made for the position of certain obstacles, which influence the fitness value. Furthermore, at this stage, the obstacles are very close to the robot, which increases the weight of the constraints and thus reduces the free space of the robot.

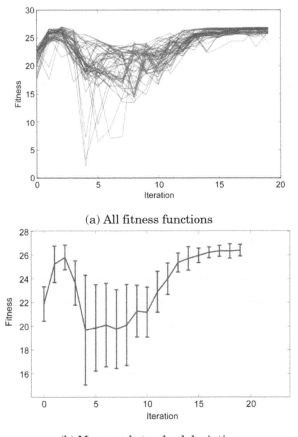

(a) All fitness functions

(b) Mean and standard deviation

Figure 3.10. *Evolution of the best individual at the second level*

At the first level, the most relevant criterion is the position error of the end effector given by the function $F1(X)$, which guarantees us that, by minimizing it, the final position chosen as the target will be reached. It is therefore interesting to follow the evolution of this criterion over generations, which is shown in Figure 3.11(a) and (b).

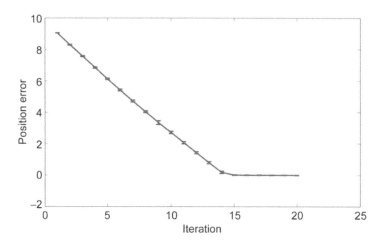

(a) Average and standard deviation

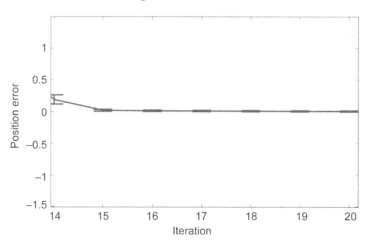

(b) Part of the curve

Figure 3.11. *End-effector position error*

As can be seen, the position error of the end effector gradually decreases over generations. Therefore, the end effector correctly reaches its final position. Also in the same figure, it can be noted that after 15 generations, the position error becomes very small. In order to conclude on the relevance of the choice of the maximum number of generations, we focus on a part of the curve between the 14th and the last generation. The result is presented in Figure 3.11(b). From this result, it can be concluded that the position error is less than 1%, which is acceptable for this configuration. This identical result reinforces the choice made about the maximum number of generations set for the first level.

Figure 3.12 shows the CPU time required to reach the final position.

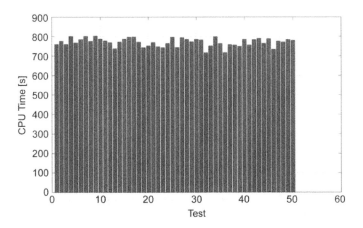

Figure 3.12. *CPU time*

As can be seen, the required CPU time is between 700 and 800 seconds for every test performed. Based on this result, it is difficult to draw objective conclusions, since it depends heavily on the chosen configuration (number of obstacles, their positions, the nature of the robot). In fact, having a large number of obstacles greatly increases the number of constraints in the proposed formulation. Much more time will therefore be required to minimize objective functions that satisfy every constraint.

Figure 3.13 shows all the configurations obtained for the robot. In this figure, it can be seen that the robot reaches its final position and avoids every obstacles located within its workspace. The dots with the symbol * represent the successive positions of the end effector. The curve shown in red represents the trajectory followed by the end effector.

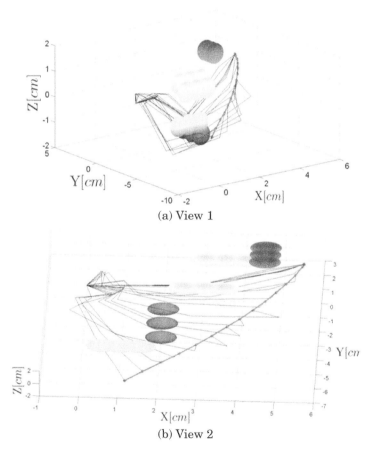

(a) View 1

(b) View 2

Figure 3.13. *Successive robot configurations. For a color version of this figure, see www.iste.co.uk/oulhadj/metaheuristics.zip*

Figure 3.14 presents two different solutions that are found by the algorithm. As can be seen, the algorithm can find two different paths to reach the final position, which is the result of the probabilistic operators implemented in the genetic algorithm. This explains the results presented in Figures 3.10 and 3.11.

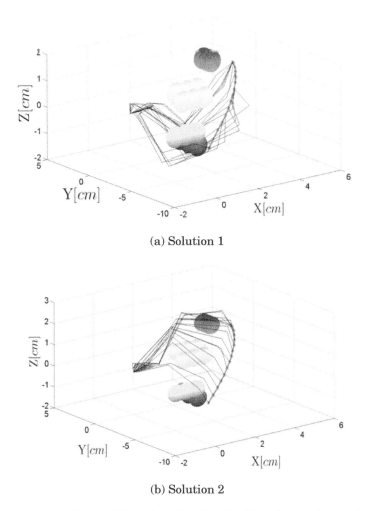

(a) Solution 1

(b) Solution 2

Figure 3.14. *Two solutions found by the algorithm. For a color version of this figure, see www.iste.co.uk/oulhadj/metaheuristics.zip*

Figure 3.15 shows the variation in joint variables for an arbitrarily chosen test.

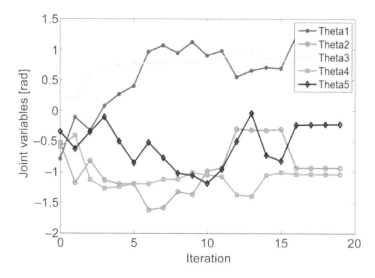

Figure 3.15. *Variation in joint variables. For a color version of this figure, see www.iste.co.uk/oulhadj/metaheuristics.zip*

From this figure, it can be seen that the oscillations due to variations in joint variables are not really significant, which prevents the robot from mechanical resonance and sudden movements that could deteriorate its structure.

The purpose of the second case under study is to show the importance of the choice of weighting parameters for objective functions. For these tests, we take $\alpha = 0.1$, $\beta = 0.2$, $\gamma = -0.7$ for the objective function of the first level and the same values for the second level. With this set of values, for the first level, more significance is given to the function $F2(\theta)$ corresponding to equation 3.4. The result is presented in Figure 3.16. As can be seen in Figure 3.16(a) and (b), the two objective functions do not converge at the end of the execution. Consequently, there is no guarantee that the end effector will reach the final position. The reason is that more significance is given to the function $F2(\theta)$. As a result, the best individual is the one with the highest value relative to this function, while its value for the function $F1(X)$ does not play a significant role. Therefore, for the proposed formulation, the choice of weighting parameters is very important, and as already pointed out in section 3.6.3, α must be greater than β and γ in order to ensure convergence.

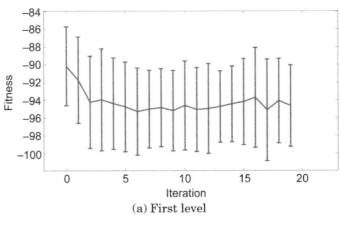

(a) First level

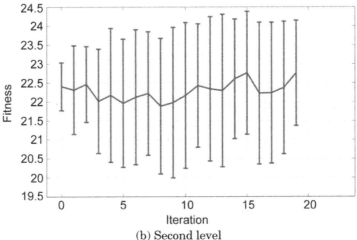

(b) Second level

Figure 3.16. *Best individual evolution. For a color version of this figure, see www.iste.co.uk/oulhadj/metaheuristics.zip*

3.7. Conclusion

In this chapter, a new method for trajectory planning for redundant manipulative arms was presented. The proposed formulation is based on the bilevel optimization approach. A metaheuristic based on genetic algorithms was used to solve the problem posed. The produced result is a set of configurations through which the robot must pass. A major advantage of this method is that it is not necessary to calculate the inverse kinematic model, which reduces the computational effort of the algorithm. Another advantage of this method is its flexibility, since it easily adapts to the number of obstacles that can be taken into account in the robot workspace.

Using performance evaluation tests, we showed the relevance of the choice of the algorithm and weighting parameters for objective functions, which play a decisive role in the quality of the final results produced. The optimal values chosen for these parameters were reinforced by testing the results. Nevertheless, the results obtained suffer from a clear lack of information on crucial data, such as the time required to reach the final configuration of the robot or the energy consumed to achieve it. In order to supplement and correct these results, the missing data will be the subject of the study presented in Chapter 4.

3.8. Bibliography

[CAL 08] CALVETE H.I., GALÉ C., MATEO P.M., "A new approach for solving linear bilevel problems using genetic algorithms", *European Journal of Operational Research*, vol. 188, no. 1, pp. 14–28, 2008.

[DAA 12] DAACHI B., MADANI T., BENALLEGUE A., "Adaptive neural controller for redundant robot manipulators and collision avoidance with mobile obstacles", *Neurocomputing*, vol. 79, pp. 50–60, 2012.

[HEJ 02] HEJAZI S.R., MEMARIANI A., JAHANSHAHLOO G.R. et al., "Linear bilevel programming solution by genetic algorithm", *Computers & Operations Research,* vol. 29, no. 13, pp. 1913–1925, 2002.

[JIA 13] JIANG Y., LI X., HUANG C. et al., "Application of particle swarm optimization based on chks smoothing function for solving", *Applied Mathematics and Computation*, vol. 219, no. 9, pp. 4332–4339, 2013.

[KUC 06] KUCUK S., BINGUL Z., "Comparative study of performance indices for fundamental robot manipulators", *Robotics and Autonomous Systems*, vol. 54, no. 7, pp. 567–573, 2006.

[LEB 06] LE BOUDEC B., SAAD M., NERGUIZIAN V., "Modeling and adaptive control of redundant robots", *Mathematics and Computers in Simulation (MATCOM)*, vol. 71, no. 4, pp. 395–403, 2006.

[LI 06] LI H., WANG Y., "A hybrid genetic algorithm for solving a class of nonlinear bilevel programming problems", *6th International Conference on Simulated Evolution and Linearing*, Hefei, China, October 15–18, 2006.

[LV 07] LV Y., HU T., WANG G. et al., "A penalty function method based on Kuhn-tucker condition for solving linear bilevel programming", *Applied Mathematics and Computation*, vol. 188, no. 1, pp. 808–813, 2007.

[ODU 02] ODUGUWA V., ROY R., "Bi-level optimization using genetic algorithm", *IEEE International Conference on Artificial Intelligence Systems*, Russia, 2002.

[PER 02] PERDEREAU V., PASSI C., DROUIN M., "Real-Time controlof redundant robotic manipulators for mobile obstacle avoidance", *Robotics and Autonomous Systems*, vol. 41, no. 1, pp. 41–59, 2002.

[POU 91] POURAZADY M., HO L., "Collision avoidance control of redundant manipulator", *Mechanism and Machine Theory*, vol. 26, no. 6, pp. 603–611, 1991.

[REN 19] RENISHAW, Neuromate robot, available at: http://www.renishaw.com/, 2019.

[SHU 13] SHUKLA A., SINGLA E., WAHI P. *et al.*, "A direct variational method for planning monotonically optimal paths for redundant manipulators in constrained workspaces", *Robotics and Autonomous Systems*, vol. 61, no. 2, pp. 209–220, 2013.

[TSA 90] TSAI M.J., CHIOU Y.H, "Manipulability of manipulators", *Mechanism and Machine Theory*, vol. 25, no. 5, pp. 575–585, 1990.

[WAN 11] WAN Z., WANG G., LV Y., "A dual-relax penalty function approach for solving nonlinear bilevel programming with linear lower level problem", *Acta Mathematica Scientia*, vol. 31, no. 2, pp. 652–660, 2011.

Metaheuristics for Trajectory Generation by Polynomial Interpolation

4.1. Introduction

This chapter outlines an interpolation method for a particular class of trajectory planning problems. The aim is to complete the method developed in Chapter 3, the results of which correspond to the best joint configurations through which the robot must pass in order to move the end effector (the terminal organ of the manipulative arm) from a starting position A to an end position B, while maintaining all of the organs of the robot away from the obstacles that clutter its environment. The disadvantage is that these results do not provide any information about the total motion time, the time required to shift from one configuration to another or the shape of the final curves. In order to better manage these aspects related to motion dynamics, it is necessary to complete the data by associating them with values on the time axis. With this in mind, the trajectory planning problem is reformalized into a constrained optimization problem, the resolution of which is based on a metaheuristic combining a *genetic algorithm* with the *augmented Lagrangian* method. The genetic algorithm is responsible for the task of optimizing the dynamic behavior of the robot and the augmented Lagrangian method is responsible for the management of associated constraints.

This chapter is organized into six sections. Section 4.2 provides a detailed description of the problem to be solved. The proposed formalization is developed in section 4.3. The solving algorithm is presented in section 4.4. Simulation results are presented with comments in section 4.5. Finally, section 4.6 concludes this chapter.

4.2. Description of the problem addressed

A trajectory can be defined in the Cartesian space or the joint space. The transition from the Cartesian space to the joint space is based on the direct geometric model of the robot, the inverse transition on the indirect geometric model. In our study, we will voluntarily assume that we are in the joint space, which has the advantage of taking into account the structure of the robot. Many interpolation techniques have been proposed in the literature [GAS 07, TIA 04, SOL 07]. They share in common the processed data, which are represented in two dimensions (2D data: the positions of the robot according to time). On the contrary, the method developed in Chapter 3 deals with data primarily described in one dimension (1D data: the positions of the robot independent of time). In order to make use of the information related to the dynamics of motion, it is necessary to complete these data by associating them with values on the time axis. At the same time, a processing method capable of processing 2D data is also needed.

To interpolate a 2D trajectory (time-based positions), two approaches can be considered:

– imposing at trajectory points a specific distribution on the time axis and interpolating it without altering the time data initially defined;

– starting from a fictitious time distribution and interpolating the trajectory while reducing as much as possible the overall time, in order to reduce, for example, the energy consumed; temporal data are considered in this case as decision variables, the optimal data of which must be found, in the same way as the missing trajectory data.

In our application (trajectory planning for redundant manipulative arms), provided that what is important is the reduction of consumed energy, the second approach will be preferred.

For the interpolation of 2D data, either trigonometric [SU 12] or polynomial [GAS 07, GAS 10, SHU 13] functions can be used. The advantage of trigonometric functions is that they have the property of being infinitely derivable, which guarantees the smoothing of the curves produced (primitive and derived curves). The disadvantage is that the input data are not easy to correct. Furthermore, a major difficulty with interpolation lies in the nature of the initial data, which can be problematic when it is necessary to reprocess them. For example, if starting nodes are too close to one another, interpolation becomes very complicated. In this case, the use of polynomial functions is more interesting because they facilitate the correction of the input data, hence the choice of this type of function. In most robotic applications, it is important to ensure smooth curves simultaneously at the position, velocity and acceleration levels. In order to meet this requirement, fourth-order polynomial functions are taken into account. Figure 4.1 shows an example of this type of curve.

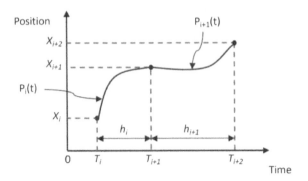

Figure 4.1. *Example of a polynomial curve*

$P_i(t)$ and $P_{i+1}(t)$ are fourth-order polynomial functions:

$$P_i(t) = a_0^i + a_1^i.t + a_2^i \cdot t^2 + a_3^i \cdot t^3 + a_4^i \cdot t^4$$
$$P_{i+1}(t) = a_0^{i+1} + a_1^{i+1}t + a_2^{i+1} \cdot t^2 + a_3^{i+1} \cdot t^3 + a_4^{i+1} \cdot t^4 \qquad [4.1]$$

To facilitate the understanding of the interpolation method developed, we will consider the simplified case of Figure 4.1, in which we have deliberately limited the number of joint variables of the robot. As shown in this figure, only the values of the angular positions X_i, X_{i+1} and X_{i+2} are initially available, which will be referred to as control nodes. These positions are assumed to be consistent with those found by the obstacle avoidance method described in Chapter 3. The objective is to find the missing 2D data of the trajectory by supplementing it by interpolation in order to optimize the trajectory at the same time as the dynamic behavior of the robot. This operation is equivalent to finding the optimal coefficients of the curves P_i and P_{i+1}, by simultaneously determining the best values of the time variables T_i, T_{i+1} and T_{i+2}. As already indicated, the trajectory in the Cartesian space will be inferred from the trajectory in the joint space based on the direct geometric model of the robot. Doing so allows the structure of the robot to be taken into account.

4.3. Formalization

As already pointed out, the problem to be solved will be formalized by only taking into account the simplified example presented in Figure 4.1.

Since each pair of successive nodes is connected by a polynomial curve separated from the following curve, it is important to ensure the continuity of the overall curve formed by joining end to end the various elementary curves that are found. This is achieved by imposing constraints at the terminal nodes of these elementary curves. The objective function to be minimized is built by linearly combining these constraints and four complementary criteria, in order to simultaneously optimize the trajectory and dynamic behavior of the robot.

4.3.1. *Criteria*

The first criterion aims to optimize the total motion time, from the starting position to the target position of the trajectory. Given that the initial data are in one dimension, the best corresponding values will be determined on the time axis by minimizing the total motion time, in order to reduce the energy consumed by the robot. The first criterion can be written as:

$$F_1(\vec{a}) = \sum_{i=1}^{N-1} h_i^2(\vec{a}) \qquad\qquad [4.2]$$

where N represents the total number of nodes under consideration; $h_i = T_{i+1} - T_i$ simulates the length of the movement time of the robot between each pair of successive nodes (see Figure 4.1); and $\vec{a}$ is the vector of decision variables composed of the coefficients of the different polynomial functions and the time parameters to be found.

In order to minimize the length of the curve, the following criterion is used:

$$F_2(\vec{a}) = \sum_{i=1}^{N-1} \dot{q}_1(\vec{a})$$ [4.3]

where $\dot{q}_i$ represents the angular velocity. For a function $y = g(x)$, the curve length is defined by equation 4.4. In order to minimize this component, the simplified expression of equation 4.5 is adopted:

$$\int \left[1 + \left(\frac{dg}{dx}\right)^2\right] dx$$ [4.4]

$$\int \left(\frac{dg}{dx}\right)^2 dx = \int \dot{q}^2\, dx$$ [4.5]

Considering the curve of Figure 4.1, $\dot{q}_i$ is the first derivative of the function P_j.

The third criterion is used to minimize ripples in robot displacements. It is expressed as follows:

$$F_3(\vec{a}) = \sum_{i=1}^{N-1} \ddot{q}^2(\vec{a})$$ [4.6]

where $\ddot{q}_i$ represents the angular acceleration. Given Figure 4.1, $\ddot{q}_i$ is the second derivative of the function P_j.

The last criterion is used to minimize the jerk, which helps to preserve the mechanical structure of the robot, by reducing actuator resonance. It is expressed as:

$$F_4(\vec{a}) = \sum_{i=1}^{N-1} \dddot{q}^2(\vec{a})$$ [4.7]

where $\dddot{q}_i$ represents the angular jerk. Given the representation of Figure 4.1, $\dddot{q}_i$ is the third derivative of the function P_j.

4.3.2. Constraints

Constraints are used to ensure the continuity of the angular curve at the control node level (pair of points marking the end of an elementary curve and the beginning of the following one). Since a polynomial function is used to individually find optimal elementary curves, it is important to ensure that the entire overall curve does not present discontinuities by joining the elementary curves end to end. Continuity conditions are therefore imposed at the position, velocity, acceleration and jerk levels according to the following constraints:

$$P_i^{\vec{a}}(T_{i+1}) = P_{i+1}^{\vec{a}}(T_{i+1}) \tag{4.8}$$

$$\dot{q}_i^{\vec{a}}(T_{i+1}) = \dot{q}_{i+1}^{\vec{a}}(T_{i+1}) \tag{4.9}$$

$$\ddot{q}_i^{\vec{a}}(T_{i+1}) = \ddot{q}_{i+1}^{\vec{a}}(T_{i+1}) \tag{4.10}$$

$$\dddot{q}_i^{\vec{a}}(T_{i+1}) = \dddot{q}_{i+1}^{\vec{a}}(T_{i+1}) \tag{4.11}$$

which represent the position, velocity, acceleration and jerk curves respectively.

These continuity constraints are reinforced by additional constraints that aim to ensure that the curve of angular positions follows as close as possible the various control nodes. For example, for the value node of the position X_i, we have:

$$\left| P_i^{\vec{a}}(T_i) - X_i \right| \leq R \tag{4.12}$$

where R is a parameter whose value is chosen to be empirically very small, in order to force the point $P_i^{\vec{a}}(T_i)$ to get as close as possible to the node X_i. Initial and final conditions are also defined. The latter involve velocity, acceleration and jerk parameters, whose initial and final values are theoretically zero.

The overall objective function to be minimized is ultimately composed of criteria 4.2, 4.3, 4.6 and 4.7. Each of them is divided by its maximal value in order to normalize this function. Given these criteria and the various constraints, the formulation of the optimization problem to be solved can be written as:

$$min \, F(\vec{a}) = \alpha . \frac{F_1(\vec{a})}{T_{max}^2} + \beta . \frac{F_2(\vec{a})}{V_{max}^2} + \gamma . \frac{F_3(\vec{a})}{A_{max}^2} + \delta . \frac{F_4(\vec{a})}{J_{max}^2} \qquad \text{[4.13]}$$

$$Under \, the \, constraints \begin{cases} Continuity \, conditions \\ Initial \, and \, final \, conditions \end{cases}$$

where α, β, γ and δ are the weighting parameters, such that $\alpha + \beta + \gamma + \delta = 1$. T_{max}, V_{max}, A_{max} and J_{max} represent the maximum allowed motion time, velocity, acceleration and jerk respectively. With the exception of T_{max} (boundary of the total motion time), which is arbitrarily chosen, the above parameters are defined by taking into account the physical characteristics of the robot.

4.4. Resolution

In the proposed formalization, there are many constraints to be met, which increase the complexity of the problem to be solved and which rise in number according to the quantity of control nodes under consideration. In effect, an increase in the number of nodes automatically increases the dimension of the search space and the number of constraints. The smoothing of the resulting curves being totally managed by the constraints, it is important to satisfy them without any exception. Finding an admissible solution that does not violate any of these constraints is a relatively difficult problem. To achieve this, the developed resolution method combines the *augmented Lagrangian* method with a genetic algorithm. The augmented Lagrangian approach helps to facilitate the management of constraints and the genetic algorithm helps to determine the optimal solution of the problem to be solved.

4.4.1. *Augmented Lagrangian*

In problems comprising a significant number of constraints, maneuvering within admissible areas becomes difficult. In order to more easily manage these constraints, the *augmented Lagrangian* method [LEW 02, CON 91, CON 92] is often used. This method allows non-feasible solutions at the start of the algorithm, but gradually converges towards feasible and optimal solutions during the iterations, which justifies its choice to solve the problem under study [SHU 13].

We will now review the general formalization of a constrained optimization problem:

$$min_x f(x) \qquad\qquad\qquad [4.14]$$

$$Under\ the\ constraints\ \begin{cases} c_i(x) \le 0, i = 1, 2, ..., m \\ ceq_i(x) = 0, i = m + 1, m + 2, ..., mt \end{cases}$$

The vector $c(x)$ represents nonlinear inequality constraints, $ceq(x)$ represents nonlinear equality constraints, m is the total number of inequality constraints and mt is the total number of considered constraints. In the augmented Lagrangian method, the constrained optimization problem is transformed into an unconstrained problem, in order to reduce its resolution complexity. It should be noted that there are several variants of the augmented Lagrangian method. A more complete description of this method can be found in [LEW 02] and [CON 91, CON 92]. The objective function of the problem to be solved can be written as:

$$F(x, \lambda, s, \rho) =$$
$$f(x) - \sum_{i=1}^{m} \lambda_i. s_i. log(s_i - c_i(x)) + \sum_{i=m+1}^{mt} \lambda_i. ceq_i(x) +$$
$$\frac{\rho}{2}. \sum_{i=m+1}^{mt} ceq_i(x)^2 \qquad\qquad [4.15]$$

where the components λ_i of the vector λ are positive and known as the Lagrange multiplier estimates. The elements s_i of the vector s are positive changes. ρ is the penalty parameter (supposedly positive). These different parameters are updated at every generation. For the iteration $k + 1$, they are updated according to equations 4.16–4.19.

At every iteration, the penalty parameter is multiplied by a factor of 10, as shown in equation 4.16. In general, the choice of this factor depends on the problem to be solved:

$$\rho^{k+1} = 10.\rho^k \qquad [4.16]$$

As indicated by equation 4.15, the vector λ, which represents the estimates of the Lagrange multipliers, is composed of two parts: the first concerns the constraints of equality; the second concerns the constraints of inequality. The part concerning equality constraints is updated according to equation 4.17:

$$\lambda_i{}^{k+1} = \lambda_i^k + \rho^k.ceq_i^k(x) \qquad [4.17]$$

As can be seen, each equality constraint has its own coefficient λ_i that is updated at each iteration, taking into account the value of the constraint in question in the previous iteration.

The update of the second part of the vector λ concerning the constraints of inequality is based on equation 4.18:

$$\lambda_i^{k+1} = \frac{\lambda_i^k.s_i^k}{s_i^k - c_i^k(x)} \qquad [4.18]$$

The vector s is updated according to equation 4.19:

$$s_i^{k+1} = \frac{1}{\rho}\lambda_i^{k+1} \qquad [4.19]$$

To calculate the new values of s, it is necessary to first update the vector λ and the penalty factor ρ.

Another important point of the augmented Lagrangian method is that it is not necessary to impose very high values on the penalty factor to ensure the convergence of the algorithm.

4.4.2. *Genetic operators*

Genetic algorithms rely on three types of operators that are adjusted over the iterations until the convergence of the algorithm. These are selection, crossover and mutation. Each of these operators comprises variations, which can lead to different results. The choice of these variants usually depends on adapting the algorithm to the optimization problem to be solved. The various operators implemented in our algorithm are described below.

4.4.2.1. *Selection operator*

This operator makes it possible to select individuals that could survive and reproduce to participate in the creation of a new generation, based on the efficiency of these individuals within a population. In our algorithm, we choose tournament-based selection.

4.4.2.2. *Crossover operator*

This operator is based on the exploration of the search space by enabling a population of solutions to progress by crossover of individuals originating from the selection step. Two-point crossover is used in our algorithm.

4.4.2.3. *Mutation operator*

Unlike the crossover operator that operates on pairs of individuals (two parents), mutation essentially operates on individuals isolated from the offspring (descendants), in order to maintain diversity within the population of solutions. The aim is to encourage the exploration of the search space in its entirety, in order to avoid premature convergence of the algorithm around a local optimum. To avoid the opposite effect, namely unnecessarily slow convergence, Gaussian mutation, with a slight adaptation explained below, is used.

In a genetic algorithm, each solution to the problem to be solved is coded in the form of a chromosome composed of a number of genes. The mutation operator operates on a few genes that are selected according to the mutation probability. In our algorithm, the selected genes are mutated according to the following operation:

$$x' = x + scale.M \qquad\qquad [4.20]$$

where M is a random variable, x represents the gene of the individual selected before mutation; and x' is the new gene obtained after mutation. For the value of M, a Gaussian distribution $M = N(0,\sigma)$ is taken, according to a normal law of mean 0 and variance σ. As explained, the purpose of the mutation operator is to promote the diversification of solutions, in order to avoid premature convergence of the algorithm. However, it is important to reduce the influence of this operator on the iterations, in order to avoid the opposite effect, namely excessively slow convergence. Hence a factor is defined which will be updated at every iteration according to the following law:

$$scale = scale - scale.\frac{current\ generation}{maximum\ generations} \qquad\qquad [4.21]$$

The overall outline of the implemented algorithm is shown in Figure 4.2.

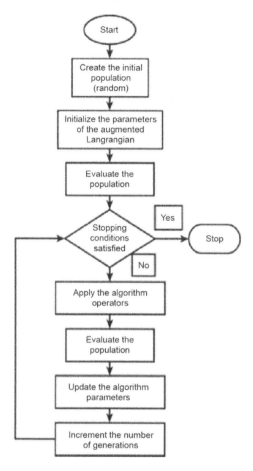

Figure 4.2. *Algorithm overall outline*

4.4.3. *Solution coding*

As previously indicated, each solution to the problem to be solved is coded in the form of a chromosome with several genes. The size of the chromosome and the dimension of the search space depend directly on the number of predefined control nodes.

In the case of the example shown in Figure 4.1, the coding of the chromosome corresponds to a sequence of parameters (genes), as shown in Figure 4.3, with $a^i \in R, T_i \in R_+^*$.

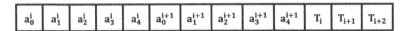

Figure 4.3. *Solution coding*

Based on the above data, the chromosome is composed of coefficients of all polynomial functions, as well as values on the time axis. For N nodes, the size of the chromosome is thus $6 \times N - 5$.

4.5. Simulation results

In order to evaluate the coding method and the algorithm developed, four control points, with angular position values *-80°, -10°, +70°* and *150°*, are predefined. Thereafter, each solution of the problem is coded with a 19-gene chromosome. Before applying the genetic algorithm, the population size, the mutation rate, the crossover probability and the tournament size are defined. The number of generations is adjusted during testing. Table 4.1 summarizes the choices made for all of these parameters.

Parameters	Values
Population size	50
Number of generations	20
Mutation rate	1
Crossover probability	0.4
Tournament size	4

Table 4.1. *Algorithm parameters*

Parameters	Values
T_{max}	20 s
V_{max}	40 deg/s
A_{max}	40 deg/s²
J_{max}	25 deg/s³

Table 4.2. *Maximum values for the variables of the objective function*

Table 4.2 gives the values of the other parameters used during the tests. The initial population is randomly set. We take $R = 5.10^{10}$ and the initial and final conditions are zero for the velocity and acceleration. To stop the execution of the algorithm, we use the maximum number of generations. The values on the time axis and the different coefficients are simultaneously found.

The objective of the first case addressed is to show the result produced by the algorithm for a choice of weighting parameters aiming to give weights virtually equivalent to all the criteria: $\alpha = 0.3$, $\beta = 0.25$, $\gamma = 0.25$ and $\delta = 0.2$. The first result of the generated curves is shown in Figures 4.4–4.6.

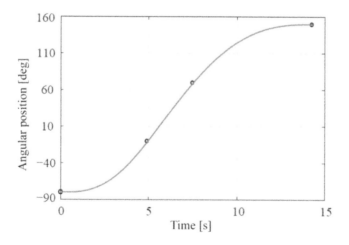

Figure 4.4. *Angular position*

At the position level, as indicated in Figure 4.4, a good result is obtained in terms of smoothing the resulting curve, which also travels through all predefined points (indicated by small black circles). It can also be noted that the total motion time (15 seconds) is much less than T_{max}.

Figure 4.5 shows the result in terms of velocity. For this variable, a very smooth curve is also obtained. Initial and final conditions are also met. In Figure 4.5, it can be observed that the maximum velocity, close to 35 deg/s, is less than V_{max}.

For the acceleration, a very efficient result is also obtained, as shown in Figure 4.6. The resulting curve is a smooth curve that respects the initial and final conditions. It can also be noted that the maximum acceleration, close to 10 deg/s^2, also does not violate the authorized A_{max} value.

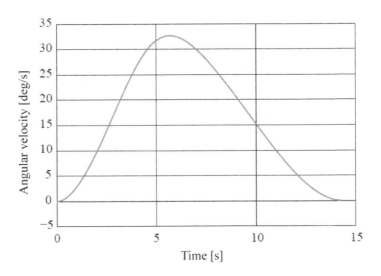

Figure 4.5. *Angular velocity*

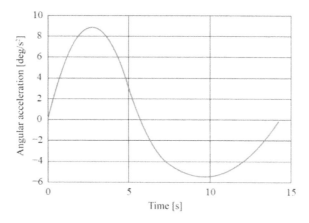

Figure 4.6. *Angular acceleration*

For the results previously presented, the algorithm was run only once. Therefore, at this stage, we cannot objectively conclude on the results produced. Since the algorithm is stochastic, it is necessary to run it several times in order to bring forward its efficiency and capability to reproduce the results. As a result, the tests are restarted by executing the algorithm several times.

The variations observed in the objective function for about 20 executions are shown in Figure 4.7.

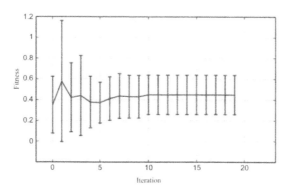

Figure 4.7. *Mean and standard deviation of the objective function*

As can be seen, the algorithm converges towards the same region. During the last generations, a mean of 0.4484 and a standard deviation of 0.3785 are obtained. It should be noted that the standard deviation is large. This is due to the incorrect setting of the parameters of the genetic algorithm and probably to the presence of local minima in the search space. Therefore, it is necessary to adjust the value of the parameters of the algorithm, in order to reduce the standard deviation and thus improve the reproducibility of the results.

Figure 4.8 shows the results for maximum velocities. As can be observed in this figure, a satisfactory result is obtained, which follows the predefined maximal value V_{max} (40 deg/s) for the majority of tests. Nevertheless, the parameters of the algorithm need to be readjusted to further refine its performance.

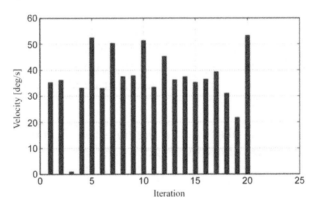

Figure 4.8. *Maximum velocities*

Figure 4.9 shows the result produced for maximum and minimum accelerations. As can be seen, all the tests are satisfactory and the predefined value for the maximum acceleration A_{max} (40 deg/s^2) is respected.

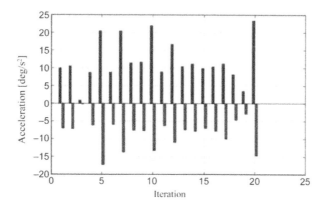

Figure 4.9. *Maximum and minimum accelerations*

Figure 4.10 shows the result obtained for the maximum jerk. It can be noted that there is only one test where the preset value for maximum jerk is violated. As a result, it can be concluded that the result is also generally satisfactory at this level.

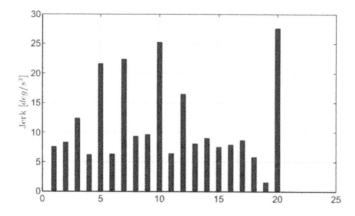

Figure 4.10. *Maximum jerk*

Figure 4.11 presents the result for the total motion time. For this parameter, the predefined value of T_{max} is also satisfied in most of the tests. In fact, it can be observed that there is only one test where this value is violated.

Another important point to check is the consumed CPU time to provide a result, which is shown in Figure 4.12. For the majority of tests, the required CPU time is less than 6 seconds, which is acceptable for the study case under consideration. This point unambiguously confirms the efficiency of the applied genetic algorithm.

Based on the results presented, it can be concluded that the choice of parameters for the genetic algorithm and of weighting parameters for the objective function, where the same significance is given to all of the criteria, have therefore led us to an acceptable performance in terms of smoothing the position, velocity and acceleration curves. By executing the algorithm several times, it has been shown that it converges towards the same region. Boundary conditions are also respected (maximum velocity, acceleration, jerk and time) in most of the cases. Another important point is that the required CPU time is absolutely acceptable.

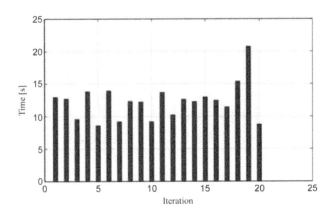

Figure 4.11. *Maximum motion time*

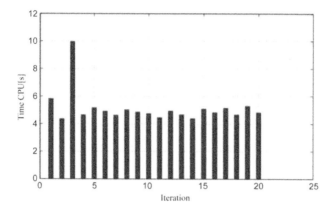

Figure 4.12. *CPU time*

The first case addressed is achieved for a choice of weighting parameters giving a weight virtually identical to all the criteria. It will be important to evaluate the behavior of the algorithm when these parameters change. The purpose of this second evaluation study is to examine the influence of these changes. Therefore, we define 20 tests in which the values of the weighting parameters are changed while keeping constant those of the parameters of the genetic algorithm. For each test, the algorithm is run 20 times and the mean and standard deviation are calculated for specific variables.

Table 4.3 summarizes the weighting parameter values for all of the tests performed. As can be observed, each test corresponds to a configuration of these parameters. For example, test 15 corresponds to the following choice: $\alpha = 0.3$, $\beta = 0.3$, $\gamma = 0.3$ and $\delta = 0.1$. For each test, we constantly keep:

$$\alpha + \beta + \gamma + \delta = 1$$

α=0.1				α=0.3			α=0.5		α=0.7		
β=0.1	β=0.3	β=0.5	β=0.7	β=0.1	β=0.3	β=0.5	β=0.1	β=0.3	β=0.1		
			Test 10			Test 16		Test 19	Test 20	δ=0.1	
		Test 8		Test 14			Test 17			δ=0.3	γ=0.1
	Test 5			Test 11						δ=0.5	
Test 1										δ=0.7	
		Test 9			Test 15		Test 18			δ=0.1	
	Test 6			Test 12						δ=0.3	γ=0.3
Test 2										δ=0.5	
	Test 7			Test 13						δ=0.1	γ=0.5
Test 3										δ=0.3	
Test 4										δ=0.1	γ=0.7

Table 4.3. *Values of weighting parameters under test*

Figures 4.13 and 4.14 show the results obtained for all 18 tests.

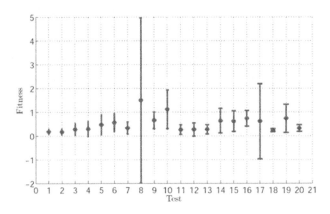

Figure 4.13. *Mean and standard deviation of the objective function after convergence*

Figure 4.13 presents the mean and standard deviation for each of the 18 tests; the results are obtained after convergence of the algorithm. We can conclude that somewhat mitigated results are achieved in terms of convergence. In effect, for test 8 (α = 0.1, β = 0.5, γ = 0.1, δ = 0.3), the standard deviation is very large compared to the results of the other tests. Test 18 (α = 0.5, β = 0.1, γ = 0,3, δ = 0.1) provides the best result. Indeed, we obtain the minimum values for the mean and the standard deviation, which shows that the population converges towards the same minimum.

Figures 4.14–4.17 show the mean and standard deviation for maximum velocity, acceleration, jerk and the total time required for the movement. The goal is to verify whether the predefined boundary values for each of these parameters (V_{max}, A_{max}, J_{max}, T_{max}) are indeed satisfied.

In terms of velocity (Figure 4.14), test 8, which produces the largest standard deviation, is also the worst test. Test 18 remains the best test, because once again it produces the smallest standard deviation.

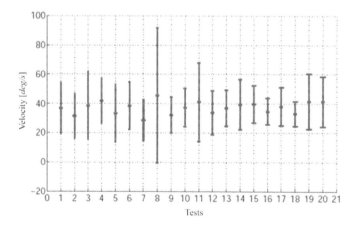

Figure 4.14. *Maximum velocity*

In terms of maximum acceleration (Figure 4.15), the results are conclusive at this level. In effect, for all of the tests carried out, this boundary value is satisfied. Based on these results, it can be concluded that test 18 is the most effective test because it produces the smallest standard deviation.

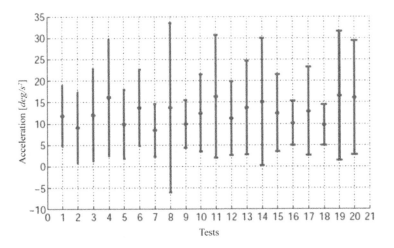

Figure 4.15. *Maximum acceleration*

Concerning the maximum jerk (Figure 4.16), the results produced do not meet the predefined maximum J_{max} with certain choices of parameters. Satisfactory results are obtained for other tests such as tests 7, 9, 16 and 18.

The final result concerns the total motion time (Figure 4.17). For this parameter, the majority of results produced are acceptable. Test 3 is the worst performing and test 20 is the most performing.

With the results previously presented, the impact of each weighting parameter cannot be analyzed independently of the others because they are interdependent. For the choice of parameter values for the genetic algorithm, it can be noted that certain configurations lead to performing results (tests 7 and 18). The results produced are trade-offs between the different criteria defined while respecting the initial and final conditions, as well as the boundaries imposed on the velocity, acceleration, jerk and total motion time.

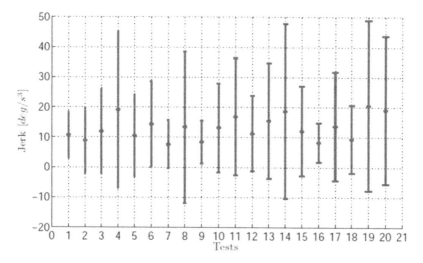

Figure 4.16. *Maximum jerk*

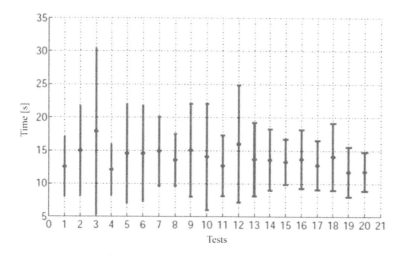

Figure 4.17. *Maximum time*

To objectively compare the interpolation method developed with competitors in the literature dealing with 2D data, it is necessary to have the same initial dataset available for all the methods involved in the competition. To this end, our algorithm is first executed in order to assign an adequate value to each control node on the time axis. The resulting 2D dataset (position of control nodes according to time) will then be used as input data for concurrent interpolation methods.

Figures 4.18–4.20 provide examples of interpolation results produced by the cubic spline method for input data corresponding to 2D nodes (0,-80°), (5.92,-10°), (7.46,70°), (15.25,150°), extracted from the results of the first study (Figures 4.4–4.6). As can be observed in these figures, continuity at different nodes is ensured for position, velocity and acceleration curves. Nonetheless, performance limitations can be observed with the cubic spline method. For the position, for example, the resulting curvature (Figure 4.18) is less significant than with the method developed (Figure 4.4). This is due to the degree of the chosen polynomial functions.

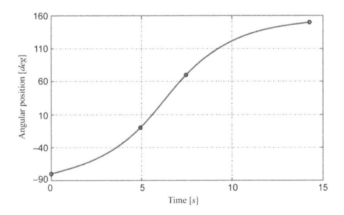

Figure 4.18. *Angular position with cubic splines*

For the velocity (Figure 4.19), it can be seen that the initial and final conditions are not satisfied by splines. For the acceleration (Figure 4.20), curve smoothing is also not satisfied by splines. This is due to the third-degree polynomials used by cubic splines. However, the initial and final conditions are indeed satisfied at this level.

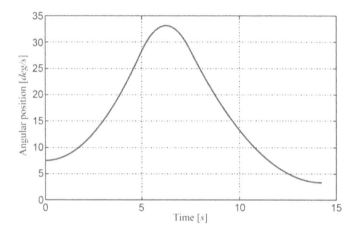

Figure 4.19. *Angular velocity with cubic splines*

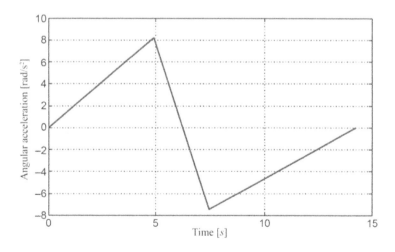

Figure 4.20. *Angular acceleration with cubic splines*

It can be concluded that the use of cubic splines must be very limited to ensure smooth curves. The other disadvantage of splines is the problem of constraint integration, such as obstacle avoidance.

Table 4.4 gives some characteristics of other trajectory planning methods, also based on interpolation operations. Method 3 corresponds to the technique proposed in [SU 12], and method 4 corresponds to that presented in [GAS 07].

Methods	Initial data	Alter the data	Boundary conditions	Smoothing
Proposed method	One-dimensional	Possible	Assured	Assured
Cubic spline	Two-dimensional	Possible	At accelerations	Position, velocity
Method 3	Two-dimensional	Impossible	At accelerations	Assured
Method 4	Two-dimensional	Impossible	Assured	Assured

Table 4.4. *Characteristics of some interpolation methods*

As can be seen, the main difference between the developed method and competitors mentioned lies in the initial data. As already mentioned, these data in our case are in one dimension (position of control nodes regardless of time). Furthermore, the values associated with these nodes on the time axis are random values that can be modified at our convenience, in order to minimize the total motion time. Using our method and splines, it is also possible to easily change the position of the control nodes, in order to keep them away from each other, for example to facilitate interpolation. This is made possible by means of the polynomial curves used by both methods. However, the data cannot be modified in the methods proposed in [SU 12] (based on trigonometric functions) and [GAS 07] (based on

B-splines). In addition, with our method and the one proposed in [GAS 07], we can easily add other conditions to the formalization, which confer them greater flexibility. With regard to smoothing the resulting curves, the cubic spline method is the only method that does not ensure smoothing at the acceleration level.

Based on the data presented in Table 4.4, it can be concluded that the proposed method has many advantages over the competing methods proposed in the literature. It is important to point out that the proposed formulation is not limited to four nodes. When the number of nodes is larger, it is necessary to duplicate continuity constraints at each of these nodes and provide a polynomial curve for each added node. For example, Figures 4.21–4.23 show the results obtained for five nodes (-80°, -10°, 70°, 150°, 200°) and the same weighting parameters ($\alpha = 0.3$, $\beta = 0.25$, $\gamma = 0.25$). As can be seen, we also achieve efficient results with curve smoothing at every level.

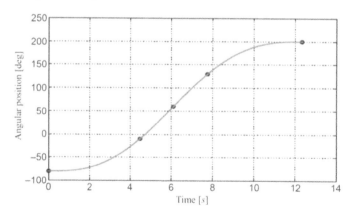

Figure 4.21. *Angular position for five nodes*

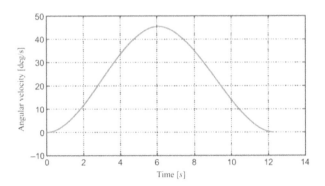

Figure 4.22. *Angular velocity for five nodes*

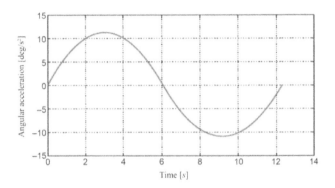

Figure 4.23. *Angular acceleration for five nodes*

4.6. Conclusion

In this chapter, an interpolation method, dedicated to a particular class of trajectory planning problems, was presented. The problem to be solved was addressed by reformulating it in the form of a constrained optimization problem. This method complements the one described in Chapter 3. Based on the implementation of a genetic algorithm combined with the augmented Lagrangian method, it provides performance results while simplifying the management of constraints, especially when these are in large numbers. In addition, it is very flexible, as new constraints can be easily integrated without changing the form of the algorithm.

The resolution of the interpolation problem makes use of fourth-order polynomial functions, which ensure optimal curve smoothing simultaneously for position, velocity, acceleration and jerk. The complexity of this method lies in the dual objective of simultaneously finding the coefficients of the various polynomials describing the elementary curves of the trajectory as well as their projections on the time axis. This complexity increases with the number of control points to be taken into account. The simulation tests carried out clearly show the efficiency of the method developed, which produces very efficient results with a small number of generations. However, as verified, the choice of parameters for the genetic algorithm and weighting parameters for the objective function has a significant impact on the quality of the results. In order to ensure the convergence of the algorithm and optimize its performance, in terms of the quality and reproducibility of its results [MEN 14a, MEN 14b, MEN 15], a detailed study was devoted to the choice of values for these parameters.

The method studied was developed with the aim of being applied in the long term in robot-assisted surgery, in order to perform interventions with optimal precision. An example of such an application is the craniotomy procedure. This procedure consists of making an opening in the cranial cap, in order to provide an access path for the surgery of the brain and its neighboring structures. This operation is composed of two stages: the first consists of positioning the end effector (the terminal point of the robotic arm) as close as possible to a specific point above a patient's head; the second consists of precisely making a hole in the skull bone.

Taking as its starting point the results of the obstacle avoidance method outlined in Chapter 3, which we want to supplement in order to optimize the dynamics of robot movements, the interpolation method developed foreshadows new applications in the field of mobile robotics for service activities in industry (logistical warehouses) and agriculture (harvesting of agricultural products) or exploration activities in hazardous environments (spatial, military, natural disasters).

4.7. Bibliography

[CON 91] CONN A.R., GOULD N.I.M., TOINT P.L., "A globally convergent augmented lagrangian algorithm for optimization with general constraints and simple bounds", *SIAM Journal on Numerical Analysis*, vol. 28, no. 2, pp. 545–572, 1991.

[GAS 07] GASPARETTO A., ZANOTTO V., "A new method for smooth trajectory planning of robot manipulators", *Mechanism and Machine Theory*, vol. 42, no. 4, pp. 455–471, 2007.

[GAS 10] GASPARETTO A., ZANOTTO V., "Optimal trajectory planning for industrial robots", *Advances in Engineering Software*, vol .41, no. 4, pp. 548–556, 2010.

[LEW 02] LEWIS R.M., TORCZON V., "A globally convergent augmented lagrangian pattern search algorithm for optimization with general constraints and simple bounds", *SIAM Journal on Optimization*, vol. 12, no. 4, pp. 1075–1089, 2002.

[MEN 14a] MENASRI R., OULHADJ H., DAACHI B. *et al.*, "Smooth trajectory planning for robot using particle swarm optimization", in SIARRY P., IDOUMGHAR L., LEPAGNOT J. (eds), *Swarm Intelligence Based Optimization*, Springer, 2014.

[MEN 14b] MENASRI R., OULHADJ H., DAACHI B. *et al.*, "A genetic algorithm designed for robot trajectory planning", *2014 IEEE International Conference on Systems, Man and Cybernetics (SMC)*, October 2014.

[MEN 15] MENASRI R., Métaheuristiques pour la planification de trajectoire des bras manipulateurs redondants. Application à l'assistance au geste chirurgical en craniotomie, PhD thesis, Paris-Est Créteil Val-de-Marne University, 2015.

[SHU 13] SHUKLA A., SINGLA E., WAHI P. *et al.*, "A direct variational method for planning monotonically optimal paths for redundant manipulators in constrained workspaces", *Robotics and Autonomous Systems*, vol. 61, no. 2, pp. 209–220, 2013.

[SOL 07] PIRES E.J.S., OLIVEIRA P.B.M., MACHADO J.A.T., "Manipulator trajectory planning using a moea", *Applied Soft Computing*, vol. 7, no. 3, pp. 659–667, 2007.

[SU 12] SU B., ZOU L., "Manipulator trajectory planning based on the algebraitrigonometri hermite blended interpolation spline", *Procedia Engineering*, vol. 29, pp. 2093–2097, 2012.

[TIA 04] TIAN L., COLLINS C., "An effective robot trajectory planning method using a genetic algorithm", *Mechatronics*, vol. 14, no. 5, pp. 455–470, 2004.

Particle Swarm Optimization for Exoskeleton Control[1]

5.1. Introduction

In the field of robotics, dynamic control algorithms generally require prior modeling of the system to be controlled. The variable tasks assigned to the robot, external disturbances, and dynamic changes related to, for example, robot wear make obtaining a reliable dynamic model for the system difficult. In practice, existing models are based on approximations, *a priori* knowledge or even simplifications of certain dynamic phenomena. When, for example, the structure of the dynamic model is assumed to be known, its various parameters and functions are determined by the identification procedure [MAJ 11]. As a whole, these models cannot accurately represent the dynamics of targeted robotic systems. This compels us to provide, among other things, robustness techniques when confronted with modeling/identification errors and also external perturbations. Several techniques have been proposed to try to overcome the disadvantages of conventional modeling. Techniques based on neural methods and fuzzy logic are examples [HSU 13, ACH 10].

---

1 This work is based largely on [BEL 17].

In addition to these methods derived from artificial intelligence, robust control techniques, based on conventional approaches or sliding mode control, have been the subject of numerous studies in the literature. Design and control systems making use of metaheuristics (genetic algorithms, particle swarm optimization (PSO)) have also been the topic of several studies [JAM 15, MEN 15a, LOU 14, CHY 12]. The effectiveness of genetic algorithms in finding the global minimum has been compared with the ease and speed of the PSO algorithm. Techniques based on PSO have highlighted two major problems. The first problem is the emergence of disrupted signals during the first search for optimal solutions. The second problem is the stagnation of the algorithm after convergence towards a single optimal solution. In the first case, particle generation is random and, since each of them provides a very different control input, the resulting signal is affected by abrupt changes before convergence to the optimal solution. In real time, this type of behavior significantly reduces the life of the system. Techniques based on conventional PSO with static optimization cannot be adapted to an optimal solution, since they remain set on the solution found during the first convergence. Genetic algorithms have a slow convergence. Consequently, they do not represent a preferred solution for controlling fast-moving robotic systems or for rehabilitation based on the use of exoskeletons [YUM 10, WEI 07, FLE 06].

In this chapter, we propose an improved and adaptive PSO algorithm for setting a PID (Proportional, Integral, Derivative) controller online. The object is an algorithm that guarantees the production of a minimum energy control signal that is minimally perturbed. This variant of modified PSO constantly searches for the optimum of the *objective* function. The proposed algorithm, when applied to trajectory tracking, can be reduced to a typical dynamic optimization problem. The applications proposed in this chapter include, among others, rehabilitation or physical assistance by means of portable robots such as exoskeleton robots [MAO 12, ZOS 06, AAR 08].

5.2. The system and the problem under consideration

5.2.1. *Representation and model of the system under consideration*

We consider an exoskeleton for the lower limb that can be used for assistance or rehabilitation purposes. The overall system, consisting of an exoskeleton and its carrier, is presented in Figure 5.1. The nonlinear differential equation [5.1] describes the dynamics of this overall system with n degrees of freedom (essentially rotational movements):

$$u = M(q)\ddot{q} + H(q,\dot{q}) - u_h \qquad [5.1]$$

where:

  – $q \in \mathbb{R}^{n\times1}$ represents the vector of joint positions;

  – $\dot{q} \in \mathbb{R}^{n\times1}$ represents the vector of joint velocities;

  – $\ddot{q} \in \mathbb{R}^{n\times1}$ represents the vector of joint accelerations;

  – $u \in \mathbb{R}^{n\times1}$ represents the vector of torques applied at the joint level;

  – $u_h \in \mathbb{R}^{n\times1}$ represents the vector of torques applied by the wearer of the exoskeleton. If the wearer does not make any effort $\Rightarrow u_h = 0_n$;

  – $M(q,\dot{q}) \in \mathbb{R}^{n\times n}$ represents the inertia matrix of the overall system;

  – $H(q,\dot{q}) \in \mathbb{R}^{n\times n}$ represents the vector that groups all the Coriolis dynamics, the friction forces as well as all other dynamics.

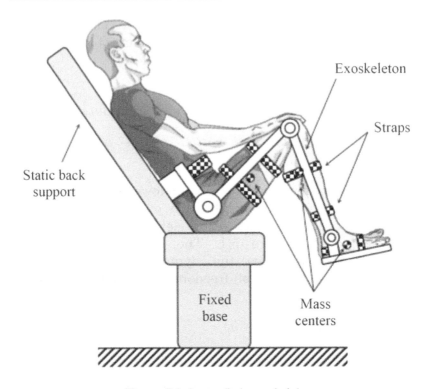

Figure 5.1. *Lower limb exoskeleton*

Generally, the functions constituting such a dynamic model (H and M) are difficult, if not impossible, to obtain by conventional modeling methods (Newton's formalism, for example). This is due, among other things, to the association of two very different dynamics (human dynamics and the exoskeleton dynamics). Even though this model is obtained, any change in real time gives a different model from what it should replicate and represent. Consequently, any control law based simply on this model may not give the desired results in terms of trajectory tracking. In this chapter, we consider these functions to be unknown and only inputs/outputs are taken into account to search online for the function that relates them. In other words, our model is of the black box type.

5.2.2. *The problem under consideration*

The problem addressed in this chapter consists of designing an adaptive control method destined for nonlinear systems whose dynamic model is considered to be unknown. Furthermore, no *a priori* knowledge is taken into account regarding this model and the controller that we propose to design must be simple and robust when exposed to external perturbations. In the literature, the authors of [LU 14] consider hypotheses about perturbations and knowledge about the dynamic model. The controller chosen in this chapter is of the PID type and its parameters are adaptive. It is assumed that the latter change in time to ensure good trajectory tracking even in the face of external perturbations.

The examples of nonlinear systems that we deal with in this chapter are exoskeletons that could be used for both rehabilitation and assistance for people with disabilities. It is therefore not easy to establish a dynamic model for the entire system composed of the exoskeleton and its carrier. Two types of dynamics must be taken into account: exoskeleton dynamics and those of its carrier. To control the entire system and ensure good performance with regard to the required safety protocol, it is important to provide robust controllers. Most controllers in the literature require that a dynamic model be established even though it is not comprehensive. Next, robustness terms are added not only to ensure proper trajectory tracking, but also to reject external perturbations, taking into account the efforts exerted by the wearer. The controller is composed of three regulated adaptive parameters that use the proposed PSO algorithm. These parameters are updated to ensure the proper performance of exoskeletons given that their use requires full compliance with the safety protocol.

5.3. Proposed control algorithm

Before presenting our approach based on the modified PSO algorithm, we believe that it is useful to conduct an analysis of metaheuristics. For a difficult optimization problem, choosing the most efficient metaheuristics capable of leading to a global optimum in a relatively short time is a crucial procedure. As a general rule, there is no theoretical method that allows the selection of a metaheuristic for a given optimization problem, except under very restrictive conditions. As a result, users remain completely dependent on their knowledge and experience when tackling a difficult optimization problem. For example, evolutionary algorithms are known for their ability to find a global minimum at the expense of high computational time and are suitable for multimodal optimization problems. The ant colony and particle swarm optimization (PSO) algorithms are better suited for dynamic optimization problems among which the optimization problem presented in this chapter can be included. The variation in the objective function over time is due not only to dynamic changes in the system under consideration, but also to the variation in the calculated control inputs. The PSO algorithm is well suited to this type of problem for its speed, its ability to approximate the global optimum and its ability to evolve in variable environments. All these properties led us to choose this algorithm for the online computation of PID parameters constituting the adaptive control.

5.3.1. *The standard PSO algorithm*

R. Eberhart and J. Kennedy proposed the PSO algorithm in 1995 [KEN 95]. It is based on the cooperation of agents, called "particles", to solve complex optimization problems by sharing information. Unlike evolutionary methods based on selection and competition, weakly performing particles are not eliminated but tend to improve their performance by using their own experience and the information received from the best particles in the swarm. The PSO algorithm represents a metaheuristic whose principle is based on a probabilistic population that is inspired by social behaviors that coexist and interact in groups [MEN 15b]. The basic model consists of a particle swarm initialized with a population of random candidate solutions. These particles move around iteratively through the search space in order to find the best solutions. Each particle is represented by a position vector X_i (where i is the particle index) and a velocity vector V_i. At every iteration, each particle remembers its best position in a vector:

$$V_i(t + 1) = WV_i(t) + T_{CR} \qquad [5.2]$$

$$T_{CR} = C_1 R_1 [P_i(t) - X_i(t)] + C_2 R_2 \big[P_g(t) - X_i(t)\big]$$

$$X_i(t + 1) = X_i(t) + V_i(t + 1) \qquad [5.3]$$

where:

C_1 and C_2 represent positive constants;

R_1 and R_2 represent random numbers taken in the interval [0, 1];

W is a variable representing the inertia factor $\in$ [0, 1].

The best position vector that minimizes the cost function within the swarm is then recorded at each iteration in a vector P_g. The velocity of each particle is also updated at each iteration depending on equation [5.2]. Thereafter, a new position is determined for every particle by adding the previous position and the new velocity according to equation [5.3].

The displacement of each particle is presented in Figure 2.4. It can be noted that the PSO algorithm is considered as an iterative method whose solution is probabilistic in nature and can be progressively reached. There are many variations in the PSO algorithm, including modifications concerning the choice of parameters, coefficients, initialization method and the choice of geographical and social neighborhoods. In order to evaluate the performance of the proposed new adaptive control algorithm, it can be compared, under the same conditions, to the controller based on a conventional PSO used in [BEL 15, BEL 16] and to the APSO proposed in [AAR 08]. Within this same context, interesting results are discussed in [BEL 17].

5.3.2. *Proposed control approach*

The approach presented in this chapter uses an adaptive PID controller with its three parameters (proportional, integral and derivative). Their values are searched for and updated using the modified PSO algorithm. The adaptive control law is given by equation [5.4]:

$$u(t) = diag\big(K_P(t)\big)e(t) + diag\big(K_I(t)\big)\int_0^t e(\tau)d\tau + \\ diag\big(K_D(t)\big)\dot{e}(t) \qquad\qquad [5.4]$$

where:

$$diag\big(K_P(t)\big) = \begin{pmatrix} K_P^1(t) & \cdots & 0 \\ \vdots & \ddots & \vdots \\ 0 & \cdots & K_P^n(t) \end{pmatrix}$$

$$diag\big(K_D(t)\big) = \begin{pmatrix} K_D^1(t) & \cdots & 0 \\ \vdots & \ddots & \vdots \\ 0 & \cdots & K_D^n(t) \end{pmatrix}$$

$$diag\big(K_I(t)\big) = \begin{pmatrix} K_I^1(t) & \cdots & 0 \\ \vdots & \ddots & \vdots \\ 0 & \cdots & K_I^n(t) \end{pmatrix}$$

$$e(t) = q_d(t) - q(t) \tag{5.5}$$

$$\dot{e}(t) = \dot{q}_d(t) - \dot{q}(t) \tag{5.6}$$

K_P^i, K_D^i, K_I^i are positive scalars calculated by the proposed control algorithm and i is an integer ranging from 1 to n;

n is the number of degrees of freedom;

t represents the time;

$e(t) \in \mathbb{R}^{n \times 1}$ represents the position tracking error;

$q(t) \in \mathbb{R}^{n \times 1}$ represents the vector of achieved positions;

$q_d(t) \in \mathbb{R}^{n \times 1}$ represents the vector of desired positions;

$\dot{q}(t) \in \mathbb{R}^{n \times 1}$ represents the vector of achieved velocities;

$\dot{q}_d(t) \in \mathbb{R}^{n \times 1}$ represents the vector of desired velocities;

$\dot{e}(t) \in \mathbb{R}^{n \times 1}$ represents the velocity tracking error.

The control scheme for the proposed adaptive approach is shown in Figure 5.2. The proposed adaptive controller based on the PSO algorithm must ensure, in finite time, the convergence of the tracking error for both position and velocity. These errors should not interfere with the operation of the system thus controlled. The *objective* function of our optimization problem is defined by:

$$f(e, \dot{e}) = \alpha \|e(t)\| + \beta \|\dot{e}(t)\| \tag{5.7}$$

with:

- $\alpha + \beta = 1$
- $0 \le \alpha \le 1$
- $0 \le \beta \le 1$

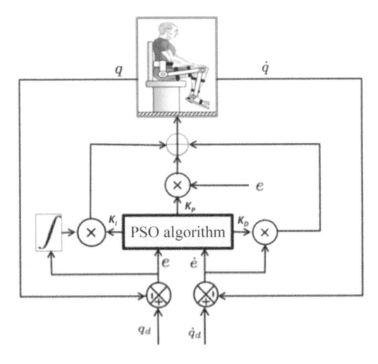

Figure 5.2. *Proposed controller*

The search space considered in our application is 3D, because the swarm is made up of m particles, each with three components corresponding to the parameters PID $(K_P(t), K_I(t), K_D(t))$. Consequently, we consider every particle as a vector PID and the goal is to find in real time the best particle that minimizes the objective function f. Organigram 1 provides the steps of the classic PSO for computing the PID components. The application of this algorithm in the field of automatic control for nonlinear systems, with an unknown dynamic model, has two major disadvantages:

1) The control signal generated by a particle in the swarm is unstable during the initial period of the search for

an optimal solution. In fact, particle generation is carried out randomly, because each gives a control value $u_i(t)$ very different from the others. The resulting signal is characterized by "chattering" phenomena during the period preceding convergence towards a single final solution. This type of behavior of the control signal generates significant vibrations and reduces the lifespan of actuators.

2) The algorithm stagnates after convergence towards a single solution, which may not be the optimal solution, especially when the system changes behavior. The current techniques based on the PSO algorithm cannot therefore be updated to the newly found solution, as they remain stuck on the previous one.

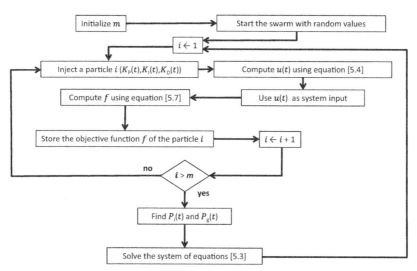

Organigram 1. *Standard PSO control*

The modified version of the PSO algorithm presented in this chapter addresses both of these problems. The idea is to generate a regular control signal with minimum energy and continue to search for a better optimal solution of the *objective* function. We deal with a dynamic function problem that incorporates changes in the behavior of the system to be controlled. It should also be noted that the automatic evaluation of a particle changes the state of the system, because each of them generates a control signal directly injected into different actuators. The proposed controller aims to perform trajectory tracking with nonlinear systems merely using their inputs/outputs and without any *a priori* knowledge about the corresponding dynamic models. As with the conventional PSO problem, we consider a randomly initialized particle swarm m in a 3D search space. Our first objective is to reduce sudden changes in the control signal, due to significant differences between particle values. The proposed solution consists of reducing the search time and ensuring a fast convergence towards a better optimal solution. To this end, we will proceed as follows:

1) Initially, particles h, such that $3 \leq h \leq m$, are used to calculate the control signal. At every iteration, each of these particles is evaluated by the objective function based on the position and velocity tracking errors. This function is represented by equation [5.7]. The convergence time is proportional to the value of h, and the stability of the control signal is inversely proportional to the value of h. However, the exploration of the search space is developed with h.

2) After the estimation of h particles, we begin the convergence of the swarm towards its three best particles, denoted by *best1*, *best2* and *best3* according to the following motion equations:

$$V_i(t+1) = \sum_{j=1} r_j C_j (best_j(t) - X_i(t)) \qquad [5.8]$$

$$X_i(t+1) = X_i(t) + V_i(t+1)$$

where r_1, r_2, r_3, are random coefficients that take their values in the interval [0,1] and C_1, C_2, C_3, are real positive constants.

Therefore, at every new evaluation of the position of a particle, we look for the three new best values and recursively apply the equations of motion for all of the swarm particles, unlike conventional PSO in which all particles are evaluated before the application of motion equations for convergence. In addition, to compute the new velocity of a particle, its previous velocity and its best performance are not taken into account. Only the three best particles of the swarm are considered. The advantage of this method is to ensure faster convergence, which provides a stable control signal. Consequently, the search space is partially explored, but a satisfactory solution is reached even though it is not the optimal solution. To improve the solution obtained without excessively degrading the control signal and at the same time to adjust the PID parameters according to the changes in the behavior of the controlled system, we propose to choose particles of k, such that $k = 10\%$ of the swarm.

These k particles (randomly selected) are used to re-explore the search space within the proximity radius of the last solution obtained after convergence of the swarm. To determine the moment of convergence, we calculate the standard deviation of the particle values. Convergence occurs when the standard deviation is below a minimum value "$ECmin$". If there is convergence and the objective function $f(e, \dot{e})$ is greater than an admissible value f_{max}, the k selected particles explore the local area in the following way:

$$X_i(t + 1) = X_i(t) + \rho \cdot R \tag{5.9}$$

where ρ is a random coefficient taken in the interval $[-1, 1]$ and R is a small search radius. We empirically adjust $R = 2$ in order to quickly adapt the control signal to changes in the system without damaging the control input too much. The objective is to respond in real time to random changes in the system, after the swarm has converged, without overworking the actuators in order to preserve their lifespan. Organigram 2 summarizes the steps of this new adaptive PID controller based on the modified PSO algorithm.

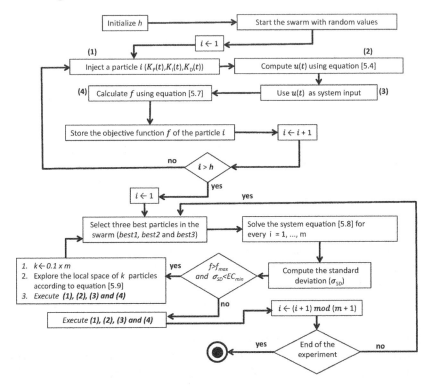

Organigram 2. *The proposed modified PSO-based control*

The results analyzed in this chapter are obtained by the application of Organigram 2 to an exoskeleton for the knee developed in the LISSI laboratory, which is called the EICoSI[2] [HAS 13, RIF 12]. For more details, in particular about the results of the simulations, see [BEL 17].

---

2 Exoskeleton Intelligently COmmunicating and Sensitive to Intention.

5.4. Experimental results

For the experimental results presented in this section, we used:

1) a PC equipped with a real-time dSpace DS1103 PPC control card;

2) Matlab/Simulink and dSpace Control Desk software.

The selected sampling period was 0.001 seconds. Figure 5.3 provides an overall illustration of the environment in which our experiments were conducted.

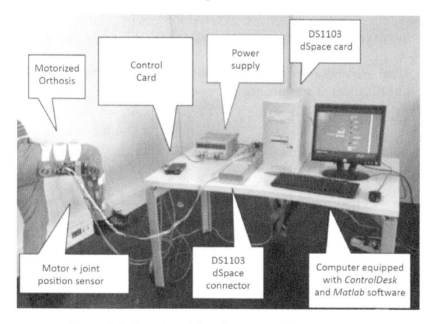

Figure 5.3. *Experimental environment [DAA 15, MAD 14]*

The exoskeleton that is the subject of our experiments is composed of two segments, with the axis of the knee aligned with the axis of the joint (Figure 5.4). The axis of the knee is driven by a DC motor-type actuator.

The system performs a synchronized movement, and the muscles acting on the knee joint exert assistive and resistive efforts on the exoskeleton. The latter generates torque, which allows for flexing/extending knee movements.

To guarantee and achieve a desired movement, our control algorithm is called upon to calculate the corresponding torque. The movements of the orthosis are constrained by those of the knee and vary between 0° and 135°, where:

1) 0° corresponds to the maximal leg extension;

2) 90° corresponds to the resting position;

3) 135° corresponds to the maximal leg flexion.

The exoskeleton under consideration may be used for rehabilitation or assistance purposes.

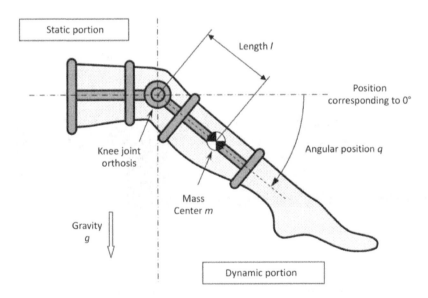

Figure 5.4. *The mechanical structure of the EICoSI [MAD 14, DAA 15, RIF 12]*

For the measurement of the actual joint position that the exoskeleton worn by an individual achieves, we used an incremental coder-type of sensor. For the joint velocity, and since we did not have any hardware sensor available to measure it, a simple derivation of the position followed by a low-pass filter was used. The purpose of using this low-pass filter was to reduce measurement noise. In concrete terms, two cases were considered in this study:

1) in the first case, the wearer was required to make no effort and remain passive, which corresponds to $u_h = 0$;

2) in the second case, the wearer was required to provide a muscular effort in the same direction as the movement (assistive effort) or in the opposite direction of the movement (resistive effort), which corresponds to $u_h \neq 0$. The desired trajectories (position and velocity), usually used to perform flexion/extension movements, are given by the following equations:

$$q_d = 1 + 0.5cos(t + \Psi)$$

$$\dot{q}_d = -0.5\,sin(t + \Psi)$$

where:

$\Psi = 60°$ for the first individual;

$\Psi = 0°$ for the second individual;

$\Psi = -15°$ for the third individual.

Three healthy individuals participated in our experiments related to the application of the proposed adaptive control algorithm. The characteristics of the participants are given in Table 5.1, and the controller parameters used are given in Table 5.2.

Individual	Size (cm)	Weight (kg)	Age	Sex	Experience
1	172	75	26	M	NO
2	178	65	25	M	NO
3	180	80	34	M	NO

Table 5.1. *Characteristics of the participants*

Parameter	Value
Swarm	Random $\in [0,150]$
Particle velocity	Initialized at 0
r_1, r_2, r_3	Random $\in [0,1]$
R	Random $\in [0,2]$
ρ	Random $\in [0,1]$
m	100
h	20
k	10
α	0.3
β	0.7
EC_{min}	0.5
f_{max}	0.5
C_1	0.8

Table 5.2. *Controller parameter values*

Figures 5.5–5.7 show the results of tracking position trajectories obtained from the three healthy individuals whose characteristics are given in Table 5.1. We can easily identify the good quality of trajectory tracking and conclude on the robustness and effectiveness of the new approach based on an adaptive algorithm relying on modified PSO. Robustness is here expressed particularly in terms of the behavior of the user who may present a resistive as well as an assistive behavior. In other words, the quality of trajectory tracking is preserved regardless of whether the user is passive or active. It should also be noted that each user has a behavior that is unique and different from any other user. The proposed PID controller is adaptive and has the ability to achieve the desired behavior in a finite and relatively short time, which does not alter the proper functioning of the exoskeleton during rehabilitation or assistance sessions when performing a variety of tasks.

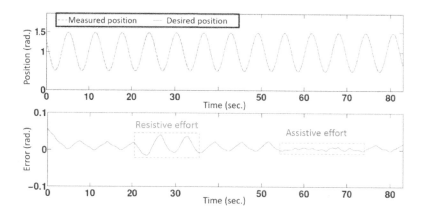

Figure 5.5. *Position trajectory tracking for individual 1. For a color version of this figure, see www.iste.co.uk/oulhadj/metaheuristics.zip*

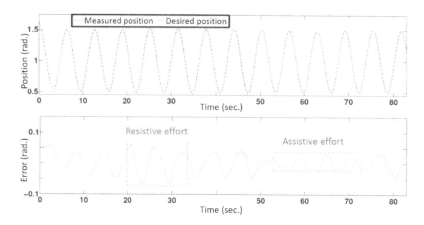

Figure 5.6. *Position trajectory tracking for individual 2. For a color version of this figure, see www.iste.co.uk/oulhadj/metaheuristics.zip*

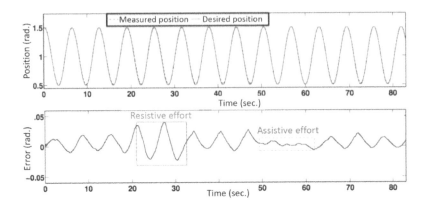

Figure 5.7. *Position trajectory tracking for individual 3. For a color version of this figure, see www.iste.co.uk/oulhadj/metaheuristics.zip*

The RMS of position tracking errors is described in Figure 5.8. Good trajectory tracking performance for the three individuals is visible in this figure. These low RMS values constitute an additional argument that clearly demonstrates the effectiveness of the proposed adaptive controller.

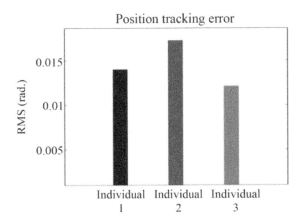

Figure 5.8. *RMS of position trajectory tracking errors. For a color version of this figure, see www.iste.co.uk/oulhadj/metaheuristics.zip*

The input control torques generated by the adaptive controller proposed for the three individuals are shown in Figure 5.9. These signals are regular with no "chattering" phenomenon and can be achieved by actuators without any problem. When resistive or assistive efforts are applied by an individual, these control signals maintain the same behavior without sudden variations. Although the three healthy subjects have a different dynamic, the controller provides in each case an achievable control input.

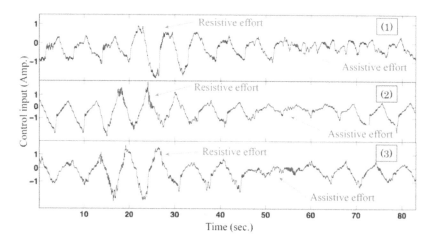

Figure 5.9. *Control inputs for the three individuals 1, 2 and 3. For a color version of this figure, see www.iste.co.uk/oulhadj/metaheuristics.zip*

The values calculated for the PID parameters, shown in Figure 5.10, are also stabilized when the objective function $f(e, \dot{e})$ is less than an authorized value f_{max}. The introduction of the resistive effort tends to increase tracking errors and therefore causes the PID parameters to vary in order to adapt the solutions to the evolution of the dynamics. Moreover, the addition of the assistive effort reduces tracking errors, allowing the algorithm to retain the same parameter values.

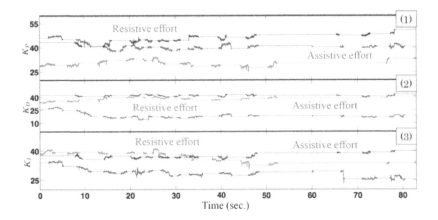

Figure 5.10. *Evolution of the adaptive PID parameters. For a color version of this figure, see www.iste.co.uk/oulhadj/metaheuristics.zip*

5.5. Conclusion

The proposed controller based on a modified PSO algorithm gives satisfactory results in terms of tracking desired trajectories. When the carrier of the exoskeleton exerts resistive efforts, the controller rejects them and maintains good trajectory tracking. On the contrary, when the carrier is able to provide assistive efforts, the control input provided by the controller is reduced on a regular basis in order to optimize energy consumption. We noted in the experimental results that there was no "chattering" phenomenon in the control signal and this could be achieved by an actuator without any problem. Compared to other controllers, the proposed controller has the advantage of giving the best results in terms of trajectory tracking and quality of control signals. In addition, the behavior of the controller in the case of external efforts is optimal and the desired performance is maintained. Since we were dealing with experimental results involving human subjects in the control loop, a precise safety protocol was followed. The three solicited users, without exception, appreciated the behavior of the proposed controller. Moreover, although the controller was adaptive and its PID parameters were initialized with random values, the convergence was so fast that it was almost impossible to detect the transient phase.

5.6. Bibliography

[AAR 08] AARON M., HERR H., "Lower extremity exoskeletons and active orthoses: Challenges and state-of-the-art", *IEEE Transactions on Robotics*, vol. 24, no. 1, pp. 144–158, 2008.

[ACH 10] ACHILI B., DAACHI B., AMIRAT Y. *et al.*, "Robust adaptive control for a parallel robot", *International Journal of Control*, vol. 83, no. 10, pp. 2107–2119, 2010.

[BEL 15] BELKADI A., CIARLETTA L., THEILLIOL D., "Particle swarm optimization method for the control of a fleet of Unmanned Aerial Vehicles", *Journal of Physics: Conference Series*, vol. 659, no. 1, 2015.

[BEL 16] BELKADI A., CIARLETTA L., THEILLIOL D., "UAVs fleet control design using distributed particle swarm optimization: A leaderless approach", *International Conference on Unmanned Aircraft Systems (ICUAS)*, Arlington, USA, 2016.

[BEL 17] BELKADI A., OULHADJ H., TOUATI Y. *et al.*, "On the robust PID adaptive controller for exoskeletons: A particle swarm optimization based approach", *Applied Soft Computing*, vol. 60, pp. 87–100, 2017.

[CHY 12] CHYAN G.S., PONNAMBALAM S.G., "Obstacle avoidance control of redundant robots using variants of particle swarm optimization", *Robotics and Computer-Integrated Manufacturing*, vol. 28, no. 2, pp. 147–153, 2012.

[DAA 15] DAACHI M.E., MADANI T., DAACHI B. *et al.*, "A radial basis function neural network adaptive controller to drive a powered lower limb knee joint orthosis", *Applied Soft Computing*, vol. 34, pp. 234–336, 2015.

[FLE 06] FLEISCHER C., WEGE A., KONDAK K. *et al.*, "Application of EMG signals for controlling exoskeleton robots", *Biomedizinische Technik. Biomedical Engineering*, vol. 51, nos 5–6, pp. 314–319, 2006.

[HAS 13] HASSANI W., MOHAMMED S., AMIRAT Y., "Real-time EMG driven lower limb actuated orthosis for assistance as needed movement strategy", *Robotics: Science and Systems Conference*, Berlin, Germany, 2013.

[HSU 13] HSU C., LIN C., YEH R., "Supervisory adaptive dynamic RBF-based neural-fuzzy control system design for unknown nonlinear systems", *Applied Soft Computing*, vol. 13, no. 4, pp. 1620–1626, 2013.

[JAM 15] JAMWAL P.K., HUSSAIN S., XIE S.Q., "Three-stage design analysis and multicriteria optimization of a parallel ankle rehabilitation robot using genetic algorithm", *IEEE Transactions on Automation Science and Engineering*, vol. 12, no. 4, pp. 1433–1446, 2015.

[KEN 95] KENNEDY J., EBERHART R.C., "Particle swarm optimization", *IEEE International Conference on Neural Networks*, pp. 1942–1948, 1995.

[LOU 14] LOU Y., ZHANG Y., HUANG R. *et al.*, "Optimization algorithms for kinematically optimal design of parallel manipulators", *IEEE Transactions on Automation Science and Engineering,* vol. 11, no. 2, pp. 574–585, 2014.

[LU 14] LU R., LI Z., SU C.-Y. *et al.*, "Development and learning control of a human limb with a rehabilitation exoskeleton", *IEEE Transactions on Industrial Electronics*, vol. 61, no. 7, pp. 3776–3785, 2014.

[MAD 14] MADANI T., DAACHI B., DJOUANI K., "Finite-time control of an actuated orthosis using fast terminal sliding mode", *19th World Congress of the International Federation of Automatic Control*, Cape Town, South Africa, 2014.

[MAJ 11] MAJHI B., PANDA G., "Robust identification of nonlinear complex systems using low complexity ANN and particle swarm optimization technique", *Expert Systems with Application*, vol. 38, no. 1, pp. 321–333, 2011.

[MAO 12] MAO Y., AGRAWAL S.K., "Design of a cable-driven arm exoskeleton (CAREX) for neural rehabilitation", *IEEE Transactions on Robotics*, vol. 28, pp. 922–931, 2012.

[MEN 15a] MENASRI R., NAKIB A., DAACHI B. *et al.*, "A trajectory planning of redundant manipulators based on bilevel optimization", *Applied Mathematics and Computation*, vol. 250, pp. 934–947, 2015.

[MEN 15b] MENASRI R., OULHADJ H., DAACHI B. *et al.*, "Smooth trajectory planning for robot using particle swarm optimization", *First International Conference on Swarm Intelligence Based Optimization (ICSIBO)*, Mulhouse, France, 13–14 May 2015.

[RIF 12] RIFAI H., MOHAMMED S., DAACHI B. *et al.*, "Adaptive control of a human-driven knee joint orthosis", *IEEE International Conference on Robotics and Automation (ICRA)*, St. Paul, USA, 2012.

[YUM 10] YUMEI M., LIJUN L., DONG N., "A note on approximation problems of neural network", *International Mathematical Forum*, vol. 5, no. 41, pp. 2037–2041, 2010.

[ZOS 06] ZOSS A.B., KAZEROONI H., CHU A., "Biomechanical design of the Berkeley lower extremity exoskeleton (BLEEX)", *IEEE/ASME Transactions on Mechatron*, vol. 1, pp. 128–138, 2006.

Conclusion

While addressing optimization metaheuristics and their application to the field of robotics, this book approaches problems based on continuous decision variables, which by their very nature may assume any value within a set of real numbers. The major difficulty to be overcome lies in the extent of the continuum of solutions to be examined in the space bounded by two arbitrary points of the search space. Theoretically, this extent is almost infinite, whether the two points are close or distant. This difficulty especially increases with the sensitivity of the objective function to the variation of the input data. In extremely sensitive conditions, very small amplitude displacements can induce considerable variations in the value of the objective function, and as a result generate solutions with completely remote effects. Given this singularity, the problems addressed can be classified into the category of optimization problems known as *NP-complete* (or *NP-hard*), for which an effective solution is very difficult to provide within a reasonable time frame using exact resolution methods based on restricted mathematical models. This explains the need to resort to optimization metaheuristics to solve them in an approachable manner, by only considering acceptable suboptimal solutions. Despite a voluntary choice that targets only a restricted field of robotics, limited to medical applications, the methods developed are generic, because they can be adapted to other optimization problems of a diverse nature without requiring fundamental modifications in the structure of algorithms. They also have the advantage of facilitating the integration of a large number of varied constraints, which would otherwise be more difficult to process by relying on limited mathematical analysis.

Compared with a range of competing methods proposed in the literature, the methods developed confirm their superiority. This reinforces the choices made to build efficiently performing algorithms, which are adapted to the problems addressed. Nonetheless, it should be noted that the quality of the results produced is strongly conditioned by adjustment of the parameters of the algorithms. Currently, this adjustment is made in most cases directly under the supervision of an expert (usually the author of the algorithm) based on a series of tests and corrections involving a test dataset related to each of the applications considered. It will be more efficient to repeat this adjustment automatically using algorithms. This will have the advantage of taking into account much larger test datasets. The larger the scope of testing data is, the more refined the performance of the optimization algorithms will be. This automatic control of the parameters can use the Monte Carlo-type trial and error method or even metaheuristics when the test dataset is too large to be able to fine-tune the results only with the Monte Carlo method.

Regardless of the approach used to adjust the parameters of the optimization algorithm (exact method, Monte Carlo or metaheuristics), two main existing methods can be used to achieve the automatic choice of parameters: *offline* adjustment before executing the optimization algorithm and *online* adjustment during its execution. In general, the offline approach results in a combination of parameters where each value is fixed completely. This approach proves effective with optimization problems where the landscape of the objective function is fairly smooth. With the online approach, the parameters of the optimization algorithm are controlled and modified throughout the iterations, depending on the estimated quality of local solutions. This approach proves effective with objective functions where the landscape is rough. On the contrary, it mobilizes a large number of computational resources, which slow down the convergence of the optimization algorithm.

Since the ideal solution does not lie in setting the parameters of an algorithm, which method should then be chosen? Clearly, there is no easy and decisive way to answer this question. Generally, manual adjustment will be sufficient if the results provided appear to be satisfactory. Alternatively, any one of the two automatic adjustment methods can be used by evaluating the quality of the desired end result and the computational effort that has to be supported. We emphasize that the automatic online parameter control approach is the method that is implemented to adjust the number of particles (solutions tested in parallel) of the PSO algorithm used in the robust control method developed in Chapter 5. Note that this parameter is increased to its maximum value when large variations are observed in the objective function. On the contrary, it is reduced to its minimum value when there is stagnation of this function. This dynamic setting makes it possible to optimize the convergence of the algorithm, in order to adapt in real time to variations in both input data and the control environment.

Another area of improvement in the works presented concerns the evaluation of the performance of the algorithms developed. For the moment, this evaluation is carried out by considering a very small number of concurrent algorithms in the literature. However, there is no common test database in the literature, at least to our knowledge, in relation to the applications that are addressed. Such a database would allow authors to evaluate their methods themselves and publish their results for comparative study purposes. It is therefore necessary to first build test datasets and reprogram each of the concurrent methods based on published algorithms. Certainly, some more or less complex test data benchmarks can be found in the literature for comparing metaheuristics. Nevertheless, these common test data are generally synthesis data, which do not reflect real practical cases. Moreover, although it is advantageous to get an initial idea of the performance of an algorithm with such benchmarks, it is not guaranteed that the algorithm will provide the same performance with real data from practical cases, which can become infinitely more complex. Furthermore, we emphasize that the results of the evaluation of the optimization methods developed correspond to the results of the studies published recently. It would be interesting to repeat this evaluation by making use of much more recent concurrent methods. Statistical tests are also needed to verify whether the performance of comparative methods is not due to chance, but is clearly dependent on their specificities and algorithmic properties.

Despite the level of performance achieved by the methods developed, further studies are clearly necessary before considering a clinical use of the results. With regard to assistance to medical procedures related to skull surgery (craniotomy), studies are underway to determine the most optimal experimental conditions to safely drill a hole into the skull cap through which surgical instruments would be introduced. It should be remembered that the manipulator arm only provides translational movements within a 3D space. The drilling of the skull bone is carried out using a machine tool whose operation and characteristics need to be optimized: the engine power, its dimensions and weight, the speed of the rotation of the drill bit, its shape and composition material. The drilling angle itself is a key parameter that should not be overlooked. For the purposes of validating the experimental protocol, trials are currently underway, involving polyamide plates whose mechanical properties are similar to those of the human skull. It would clearly be necessary to extend these trials to guinea pigs (wild and domestic animals) before considering such a surgical procedure on a human subject. Obviously, the goal is not to replace practitioners by a machine, no matter how intelligent it would be, but to assist them in their tasks, in order to increase their efficiency by improving the precision of the surgical procedure in particular. For safety reasons, this type of procedure would permanently take place under the watchful eye of the surgeon, who could regain control at any time if necessary.

Concerning adaptive control for effort assistance, experimental tests are still needed to best optimize the functioning of the exoskeleton. For example, it is important to improve the ergonomics of the system and minimize the energy consumption required to operate it. Reducing the risk of the system runaway condition is also crucial. All these improvements are necessary before it is possible to guarantee that the assisting system is hazard-free and safe for the user. Evaluation studies will therefore continue as long as necessary, in order to optimize the performance of the assisting system as much as possible.

Finally, we emphasize again that the study presented is the result of work in academic research. This book would not be complete without gratefully mentioning all those who directly or indirectly participated in the work carried out: trainees, technicians, doctoral students, as well as all university and hospital supervisors. We will not forget everyone who contributed to this book by reviewing, revising and correcting the text and the final version of the manuscript.

Index

Other titles from

in

Computer Engineering

2019

BESBES Walid, DHOUIB Diala, WASSAN Niaz, MARREKCHI Emna
Solving Transport Problems: Towards Green Logistics

CLERC Maurice
Iterative Optimizers: Difficulty Measures and Benchmarks

GHLALA Riadh
Analytic SQL in SQL Server 2014/2016

TOUNSI Wiem
Cyber-Vigilance and Digital Trust: Cyber Security in the Era of Cloud Computing and IoT

2018

ANDRO Mathieu
Digital Libraries and Crowdsourcing
(Digital Tools and Uses Set – Volume 5)

ARNALDI Bruno, GUITTON Pascal, MOREAU Guillaume
Virtual Reality and Augmented Reality: Myths and Realities

BERTHIER Thierry, TEBOUL Bruno
From Digital Traces to Algorithmic Projections

CARDON Alain
Beyond Artificial Intelligence: From Human Consciousness to Artificial Consciousness

HOMAYOUNI S. Mahdi, FONTES Dalila B.M.M.
Metaheuristics for Maritime Operations
(Optimization Heuristics Set – Volume 1)

JEANSOULIN Robert
JavaScript and Open Data

PIVERT Olivier
NoSQL Data Models: Trends and Challenges
(Databases and Big Data Set – Volume 1)

SEDKAOUI Soraya
Data Analytics and Big Data

SALEH Imad, AMMI Mehdi, SZONIECKY Samuel
Challenges of the Internet of Things: Technology, Use, Ethics
(Digital Tools and Uses Set – Volume 7)

SZONIECKY Samuel
Ecosystems Knowledge: Modeling and Analysis Method for Information and Communication
(Digital Tools and Uses Set – Volume 6)

2017

BENMAMMAR Badr
Concurrent, Real-Time and Distributed Programming in Java

HÉLIODORE Frédéric, NAKIB Amir, ISMAIL Boussaad, OUCHRAA Salma, SCHMITT Laurent
Metaheuristics for Intelligent Electrical Networks
(Metaheuristics Set – Volume 10)

MA Haiping, SIMON Dan
Evolutionary Computation with Biogeography-based Optimization
(Metaheuristics Set – Volume 8)

PÉTROWSKI Alain, BEN-HAMIDA Sana
Evolutionary Algorithms
(Metaheuristics Set – Volume 9)

PAI G A Vijayalakshmi
Metaheuristics for Portfolio Optimization
(Metaheuristics Set – Volume 11)

2016

BLUM Christian, FESTA Paola
Metaheuristics for String Problems in Bio-informatics
(Metaheuristics Set – Volume 6)

DEROUSSI Laurent
Metaheuristics for Logistics
(Metaheuristics Set – Volume 4)

DHAENENS Clarisse and JOURDAN Laetitia
Metaheuristics for Big Data
(Metaheuristics Set – Volume 5)

LABADIE Nacima, PRINS Christian, PRODHON Caroline
Metaheuristics for Vehicle Routing Problems
(Metaheuristics Set – Volume 3)

LEROY Laure
Eyestrain Reduction in Stereoscopy

LUTTON Evelyne, PERROT Nathalie, TONDA Albert
Evolutionary Algorithms for Food Science and Technology
(Metaheuristics Set – Volume 7)

MAGOULÈS Frédéric, ZHAO Hai-Xiang
Data Mining and Machine Learning in Building Energy Analysis

RIGO Michel
Advanced Graph Theory and Combinatorics

2015

BARBIER Franck, RECOUSSINE Jean-Luc
COBOL Software Modernization: From Principles to Implementation with the BLU AGE® Method

CHEN Ken
Performance Evaluation by Simulation and Analysis with Applications to Computer Networks

CLERC Maurice
Guided Randomness in Optimization
(Metaheuristics Set – Volume 1)

DURAND Nicolas, GIANAZZA David, GOTTELAND Jean-Baptiste, ALLIOT Jean-Marc
Metaheuristics for Air Traffic Management
(Metaheuristics Set – Volume 2)

MAGOULÈS Frédéric, ROUX François-Xavier, HOUZEAUX Guillaume
Parallel Scientific Computing

MUNEESAWANG Paisarn, YAMMEN Suchart
Visual Inspection Technology in the Hard Disk Drive Industry

2014

BOULANGER Jean-Louis
Formal Methods Applied to Industrial Complex Systems

BOULANGER Jean-Louis
Formal Methods Applied to Complex Systems:
Implementation of the B Method

GARDI Frédéric, BENOIST Thierry, DARLAY Julien, ESTELLON Bertrand, MEGEL Romain
Mathematical Programming Solver based on Local Search

BOULANGER Jean-Louis
Safety Management for Software-based Equipment

DELAHAYE Daniel, PUECHMOREL Stéphane
Modeling and Optimization of Air Traffic

FRANCOPOULO Gil
LMF — Lexical Markup Framework

GHÉDIRA Khaled
Constraint Satisfaction Problems

ROCHANGE Christine, UHRIG Sascha, SAINRAT Pascal
Time-Predictable Architectures

WAHBI Mohamed
Algorithms and Ordering Heuristics for Distributed Constraint Satisfaction
Problems

ZELM Martin *et al.*
Enterprise Interoperability

2012

ARBOLEDA Hugo, ROYER Jean-Claude
Model-Driven and Software Product Line Engineering

BLANCHET Gérard, DUPOUY Bertrand
Computer Architecture

BOULANGER Jean-Louis
Industrial Use of Formal Methods: Formal Verification

BOULANGER Jean-Louis
Formal Method: Industrial Use from Model to the Code

CALVARY Gaëlle, DELOT Thierry, SÈDES Florence, TIGLI Jean-Yves
Computer Science and Ambient Intelligence

MAHOUT Vincent
*Assembly Language Programming: ARM Cortex-M3 2.0: Organization,
Innovation and Territory*

MARLET Renaud
Program Specialization

SOTO Maria, SEVAUX Marc, ROSSI André, LAURENT Johann
Memory Allocation Problems in Embedded Systems: Optimization Methods

2011

BICHOT Charles-Edmond, SIARRY Patrick
Graph Partitioning

BOULANGER Jean-Louis
Static Analysis of Software: The Abstract Interpretation

CAFERRA Ricardo
Logic for Computer Science and Artificial Intelligence

HOMES Bernard
Fundamentals of Software Testing

KORDON Fabrice, HADDAD Serge, PAUTET Laurent, PETRUCCI Laure
Distributed Systems: Design and Algorithms

KORDON Fabrice, HADDAD Serge, PAUTET Laurent, PETRUCCI Laure
Models and Analysis in Distributed Systems

LORCA Xavier
Tree-based Graph Partitioning Constraint

TRUCHET Charlotte, ASSAYAG Gerard
Constraint Programming in Music

VICAT-BLANC PRIMET Pascale *et al.*
Computing Networks: From Cluster to Cloud Computing

2010

AUDIBERT Pierre
Mathematics for Informatics and Computer Science

BABAU Jean-Philippe *et al.*
Model Driven Engineering for Distributed Real-Time Embedded Systems

BOULANGER Jean-Louis
Safety of Computer Architectures

MONMARCHE Nicolas *et al.*
Artificial Ants

PANETTO Hervé, BOUDJLIDA Nacer
Interoperability for Enterprise Software and Applications 2010

SIGAUD Olivier *et al.*
Markov Decision Processes in Artificial Intelligence

SOLNON Christine
Ant Colony Optimization and Constraint Programming

AUBRUN Christophe, SIMON Daniel, SONG Ye-Qiong *et al.*
Co-design Approaches for Dependable Networked Control Systems

2009

FOURNIER Jean-Claude
Graph Theory and Applications

GUEDON Jeanpierre
The Mojette Transform / Theory and Applications

JARD Claude, ROUX Olivier
Communicating Embedded Systems / Software and Design

LECOUTRE Christophe
Constraint Networks / Targeting Simplicity for Techniques and Algorithms

2008

BANÂTRE Michel, MARRÓN Pedro José, OLLERO Hannibal, WOLITZ Adam
Cooperating Embedded Systems and Wireless Sensor Networks

MERZ Stephan, NAVET Nicolas
Modeling and Verification of Real-time Systems

PASCHOS Vangelis Th
Combinatorial Optimization and Theoretical Computer Science: Interfaces and Perspectives

WALDNER Jean-Baptiste
Nanocomputers and Swarm Intelligence

2007

BENHAMOU Frédéric, JUSSIEN Narendra, O'SULLIVAN Barry
Trends in Constraint Programming

JUSSIEN Narendra
A TO Z OF SUDOKU

2006

BABAU Jean-Philippe *et al.*
From MDD Concepts to Experiments and Illustrations – DRES 2006

HABRIAS Henri, FRAPPIER Marc
Software Specification Methods

MURAT Cecile, PASCHOS Vangelis Th
Probabilistic Combinatorial Optimization on Graphs

PANETTO Hervé, BOUDJLIDA Nacer
Interoperability for Enterprise Software and Applications 2006 / IFAC-IFIP I-ESA'2006

2005

GÉRARD Sébastien *et al.*
Model Driven Engineering for Distributed Real Time Embedded Systems

PANETTO Hervé
Interoperability of Enterprise Software and Applications 2005

Printed and bound by CPI Group (UK) Ltd, Croydon, CR0 4YY